5646

D0075795

DATE DUE

26 '91			
MAR 11 '92			
26 '92			
JUL 23 '92			
JUN 8 '93			
JUN 17 '93			

HIGHSMITH 45-220

NEW ESSAYS ON THE GREAT GATSBY

★ The American Novel ★

Emory Elliott, *Princeton University*

Other books in the series:
New Essays on The Scarlet Letter
New Essays on Adventures of Huckleberry Finn

Forthcoming:
New Essays on Chopin's The Awakening (ed. Wendy Martin)
New Essays on The Red Badge of Courage (ed. Lee Mitchell)
New Essays on Ellison's Invisible Man (ed. Robert O'Meally)
New Essays on Light in August (ed. Michael Millgate)
New Essays on The Sun Also Rises (ed. Linda Wagner)
New Essays on James's The American (ed. Martha Banta)
New Essays on Moby-Dick (ed. Richard Brodhead)
New Essays on Uncle Tom's Cabin (ed. Eric Sundquist)

New Essays on
The Great Gatsby

Edited by
Matthew J. Bruccoli

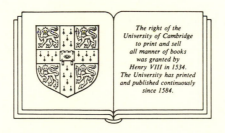

The right of the
University of Cambridge
to print and sell
all manner of books
was granted by
Henry VIII in 1534.
The University has printed
and published continuously
since 1584.

CAMBRIDGE UNIVERSITY PRESS

Cambridge

London   New York   New Rochelle

Melbourne   Sydney

Published by the Press Syndicate of the University of Cambridge
The Pitt Building, Trumpington Street, Cambridge CB2 1RP
32 East 57th Street, New York, NY 10022, USA
10 Stamford Road, Oakleigh, Melbourne 3166, Australia

First Published 1985
Reprinted 1986, 1987

Printed in the United States of America

Library of Congress Cataloging in Publication Data
Main entry under title:
New essays on The great Gatsby.

(The American novel)
Bibliography: p.
1. Fitzgerald, F. Scott (Francis Scott), 1896–1940.
Great Gatsby—Addresses, essays, lectures. I. Bruccoli,
Matthew Joseph, 1931–   . II. Series.
PS3511.I9G866 1985 813'.52 85–7823
ISBN 0 521 26589 4 hard covers
ISBN 0 521 31963 3 paperback

Contents

Contents

Series Editor's Preface

IN literary criticism the last twenty-five years have been particularly fruitful. Since the rise of the New Criticism in the 1950s, which focused attention of critics and readers upon the text itself – apart from history, biography, and society – there has emerged a wide variety of critical methods which have brought to literary works a rich diversity of perspectives: social, historical, political, psychological, economic, ideological, and philosophical. While attention to the text itself, as taught by the New Critics, remains at the core of contemporary interpretation, the widely shared assumption that works of art generate many different kinds of interpretation has opened up possibilities for new readings and new meanings.

Before this critical revolution, many American novels had come to be taken for granted by earlier generations of readers as having an established set of recognized interpretations. There was a sense among many students that the canon was established and that the larger thematic and interpretative issues had been decided. The task of the new reader was to examine the ways in which elements such as structure, style, and imagery contributed to each novel's acknowledged purpose. But recent criticism has brought these old assumptions into question and has thereby generated a wide variety of original, and often quite surprising, interpretations of the classics, as well as of rediscovered novels such as Kate Chopin's *The Awakening*, which has only recently entered the canon of works that scholars and critics study and that teachers assign their students.

The aim of The American Novel Series is to provide students of American literature and culture with introductory critical guides to

American novels now widely read and studied. Each volume is devoted to a single novel and begins with an introduction by the volume editor, a distinguished authority on the text. The introduction presents details of the novel's composition, publication history, and contemporary reception, as well as a survey of the major critical trends and readings from first publication to the present. This overview is followed by four or five original essays, specifically commissioned from senior scholars of established reputation and from outstanding younger critics. Each essay presents a distinct point of view, and together they constitute a forum of interpretative methods and of the best contemporary ideas on each text.

It is our hope that these volumes will convey the vitality of current critical work in American literature, generate new insights and excitement for students of the American novel, and inspire new respect for and new perspectives upon these major literary texts.

Emory Elliott
Princeton University

1

Introduction

MATTHEW J. BRUCCOLI

1

THE charge that F. Scott Fitzgerald was an irresponsible writer is refuted by the compositional history of *The Great Gatsby*. He began planning the novel during the summer of 1922 as a work set in the Midwest and New York at the end of the nineteenth century. At that time he announced to Maxwell Perkins, his editor: "I want to write something *new* — something extraordinary and beautiful and simple + intricately patterned."[1] He started writing an early version of the novel in the summer of 1923 at Great Neck, Long Island, the locale for the published novel, but serious work did not commence until the summer of 1924 on the Riviera. The typescript was sent to Perkins in November. Prompted by his editor's response, Fitzgerald rewrote and restructured the novel in galley proof during January and February 1925 in Rome.[2]

The rewritten proofs were dispatched to Perkins with Fitzgerald's report that he had solved the problems that bothered both of them:

(1.) I've brought Gatsby to life
(2.) I've accounted for his money
(3.) I've fixed up the two weak chapters (VI and VII)
(4.) I've improved his first party
(5.) I've broken up his long narrative in Chap. VIII[3]

Gatsby achieved its greatness in proof. Fitzgerald's principal concern was to improve the existing narrative plan by shifting the pieces of Gatsby's biography: Gatsby's revelation to Nick of his love for Daisy (originally in Chapter Seven) and the account of Dan Cody and Gatsby (originally in Chapter Eight) were incorporated into Chapter Six. The novel is a work of genius, but it is equally a triumph of craftsmanship.

2

In 1925 Fitzgerald's short novel about a flamboyant racketeer's attempt to recapture the upper-class girl who threw him over seemed an unlikely candidate for masterpiece or world-classic stature. It was a commercial disappointment when it was published in April 1925; the two printings that year totaled 23,870 copies. (*This Side of Paradise* had sold 41,075 copies in 1920.)* Yet the reviews included the warmest Fitzgerald had received – along with some opaque dismissals. Gilbert Seldes announced that "Fitzgerald has more than matured; he has mastered his talent and gone soaring in a beautiful flight, leaving behind him everything dubious and tricky in his earlier work, and leaving even farther behind all the men of his own generation and most of his elders."[4] This review appeared late in *The Dial*, a small-circulation literary journal. In January 1926, Seldes complained in the English *New Criterion* that the reviews had not been sufficiently enthusiastic, saying that Fitzgerald "stands at this time desperately in need of critical encouragement."[5] Among the prominent receptive critics were William Rose Benet in *The Saturday Review of Literature*, Laurence Stallings in the *New York World* (after an earlier unsigned *World* review was headlined "F. Scott Fitzgerald's Latest a Dud"), Herbert S. Gorman in the *New York Sun*, Harry Hansen in the *Chicago Daily News*, Carl Van Vechten in *The Nation*, and Herschel Brickell in the *New York Evening Post*. Probably the review that most concerned the author was H. L. Mencken's long piece in the *Baltimore Evening Sun*, which expressed reservations about the novel while recognizing Fitzgerald's development as a writer:

*The best-selling novels of 1925 were *Soundings* by A. Hamilton Gibbs, *The Constant Nymph* by Margaret Kennedy, *The Keeper of the Bees* by Gene Stratton Porter, *Glorious Apollo* by E. Barrington, *The Green Hat* by Michael Arlen, *The Little French Girl* by Anne Douglas Sedgwick, *Arrowsmith* by Sinclair Lewis, *The Perennial Bachelor* by Anne Parish, *The Carolinian* by Rafael Sabatini, and *Our Increasing Purpose* by A. S. M. Hutchinson.

The story is obviously unimportant . . . it is certainly not to be put on the same shelf with, say, *This Side of Paradise.* What ails it, fundamentally, is the plain fact that it is simply a story – that Fitzgerald seems to be far more interested in maintaining its suspense than in getting under the skins of its people. It is not that they are false; it is that they are taken too much for granted. Only Gatsby himself genuinely lives and breathes. The rest are mere marionettes – often astonishingly lifelike, but nevertheless not quite alive.

What gives the story distinction is something quite different from the management of the action or the handling of the characters; it is the charm and beauty of the writing.[6]

Charles Scribner's Sons made a strong effort to promote the book. It was packaged in a striking dust jacket by Francis Cugat, but the jacket copy conveys the impression that the publisher was uncertain about the nature of its product: "It is a magical, living book, blended of irony, romance, and mysticism." The seven ads in *The Saturday Review of Literature* from April to June indicate that Scribners allocated a generous advertising budget to *The Great Gatsby.* The second ad (April 25) was captioned "F. Scott Fitzgerald, Satirist," indicating that the publisher was still looking for the right handle.[7] The fifth ad (May 23) announced:

> *"Mencken is*
> *right:"*
> says JOSEPH
> HERGESHEIMER
> *"it is beautifully*
> *written and satu-*
> *rated with a sharp,*
> *unforgettable emo-*
> *tion. It gathers up*
> *all his early prom-*
> *ise surprisingly*
> *soon, and what he*
> *subsequently does*
> *must be of great*
> *interest and importance."*[8]

The English impact was negligible. The 1926 Chatto & Windus printing did not sell well, although the reviews were better than those Fitzgerald's previous novels had received in England. The *Times Literary Supplement* called it "undoubtedly a work of art and of great promise"; Edward Shanks in the *London Mercury* commended the author's control over his material. Conrad Aiken, writing in *The New Criterion,* praised the form and originality of the novel but stated that it is not "great," "large," or "strikingly subtle." L. P. Hartley called it "an absurd story" in the *Saturday Review.*[9]

The novel was dead in the market before the end of 1925, even though *The Great Gatsby* achieved exposure through the 1926 dramatization by Owen Davis that ran for 112 performances on Broadway and the 1926 silent movie based on the play. This publicity did not sell the book. Copies of the August 1925 second printing were still in the warehouse when Fitzgerald died in 1940. There was one more American printing during the author's lifetime, the 1934 Modern Library volume — discontinued for lack of sales. This reprint added Fitzgerald's introduction replying to the charges of triviality brought against his work in the proletarian thirties: "But, my God! it was my material, and it was all I had to deal with."[10] The only other republications of *Gatsby* during Fitzgerald's lifetime were in two pulp magazines: *Famous Story Magazine* serialized it in 1926, and the English *Argosy* ran it in one 1937 issue.

Fitzgerald's newspaper obituaries revealed no awareness that *The Great Gatsby* was more than a period piece. The *New York Times* devoted a paragraph to the novel:

> The best of his books, the critics said, was *The Great Gatsby.* When it was published in 1925 this ironic tale of life on Long Island at a time when gin was the national drink and sex the national obsession (according to the exponents of Mr. Fitzgerald's school of writers), it received critical acclaim. In it Mr. Fitzgerald was at his best, which was, according to John Chamberlain, "his ability to catch . . . the flavor of a period, the fragrance of a night, a snatch of old song, in a phrase."[11]

The next day, an editorial stated: "It was not a book for the ages, but it caught superbly the spirit of a decade."[12] James Gray wrote "A Last Salute to the Gayest of Sad Young Men" for the *St. Paul Dispatch* in which he ventured the "heresy" that the Nobel Prize had been awarded to writers who had not produced anything as brilliant as *The Great Gatsby:* "Perhaps some day it will be rediscovered."[13] *The New Yorker's* comment on the obituaries described *Gatsby* as "one of the most scrupulously observed and beautifully written of American novels."[14]

The 1941 assessments and tributes generally played it safe by viewing Fitzgerald as a writer who had failed to fulfill his promise. Even in the series of reminiscences that appeared in two 1941 issues of *The New Republic,* John Peale Bishop's elegy lamented Fitzgerald's failure. The other contributors included Malcolm Cowley, John Dos Passos, John O'Hara, Budd Schulberg, and Glenway Wescott. Dos Passos challenged the nostalgia or period-flavor critical approach to Fitzgerald and declared that *Gatsby* was "one of the few classic American novels."[15]

Fitzgerald's death triggered a *Gatsby* revival – which triggered the Fitzgerald revival. Unlike the Melville revival, which was the work of academics, the Fitzgerald revival was a popular response resulting from reader demand in the forties. Critical reassessment of the novel was mainly a process of the fifties.[16] During the forties no article devoted to *The Great Gatsby* was published, but there were appraisals or reappraisals of Fitzgerald that singled it out for praise. In 1945 William Troy identified *Gatsby* as Fitzgerald's only completely successful novel, and in 1946 John Berryman declared it a "masterpiece."[17]

Publishers did more than the critics for Fitzgerald. Between 1941 and 1949, seventeen new editions or reprints of *The Great Gatsby* were published. The key event was the inclusion of *Gatsby* with *The Last Tycoon* in 1941, for the respectful posthumous attention attracted by the unfinished novel carried over to *Gatsby*. In 1942 Scribners brought out a small reprint of *Gatsby*.

Three years later, the novel became widely available and widely sold – the surest gauge of a book's influence. In 1945 there were five new editions or reprints – as well as *The Crack-Up,* with its section of letters about *Gatsby* from Edith Wharton, T. S. Eliot, and Gertrude Stein. That year the *Tycoon/Gatsby* edition went into a second printing, the Armed Services Edition was published, the *Viking Portable* Fitzgerald (which included *Gatsby* and *Tender Is the Night*) was published and required a second printing, and the twenty-five-cent Bantam paperback was released. It is impossible to determine the effect of a book giveaway program, but publishing historians have credited the 155,000 copies (nearly eight times the 1925 first printing) of the Armed Services Edition distributed to military personnel with creating a new readership for *The Great Gatsby*.

In 1946 the Bantam paperback was reprinted twice, New Directions published *Gatsby* in the New Classics series – with an introduction by Lionel Trilling – and *Gatsby* was included in *Great American Short Novels* (four printings in the forties). The *Portable* went into third and fourth printings in 1949, and that year Grosset & Dunlap brought out a tie-in printing for the Alan Ladd movie version.

Before *The Great Gatsby* became a required textbook in the fifties and sixties, some half million copies were in the hands of readers who were reading it because they wanted to read it.

3

For a long time, *The Great Gatsby* was classified as "a book about the Roaring Twenties." It is one of those novels that so richly evoke the texture of their time that they become, in the fullness of time, more than literary classics; they become a supplementary or even substitute form of history. It is surprising that this statement should apply to a work by F. Scott Fitzgerald, for in certain ways the historiographer of the Jazz Age (which he named) was ill-equipped for the task.

He was not a documentary writer. John O'Hara paid him the tribute of declaring: "He always knew what he was writing about. . . . Scott Fitzgerald had the correct impressions because, quite apart from his gifts, the impressions were not those of a man who's never been there."[18] Although O'Hara carefully repeated the word "impressions," the implication that Fitzgerald was a master reporter is overgenerous. His control of detail was never as sharp or comprehensive as O'Hara's. The most famous car in American fiction is never identified. Fitzgerald may have felt that to stipulate its make would render the "circus wagon"/"death car" less extraordinary – it would have become just a Pierce-Arrow or Stutz or Duesenberg. Instead, he treated the vehicle impressionistically: "It was a rich cream color, bright with nickel, swollen here and there in its monstrous length with triumphant hat-boxes and supper-boxes and tool boxes, terraced with a labyrinth of wind-shields that mirrored a dozen suns" (p. 77).† He relied on style to evoke a car appropriate for Gatsby. (Note Fitzgerald's characteristic use of the surprising adjective in "*triumphant* hat-boxes.")

The Great Gatsby provides little in the way of sociological or anthropological data. Three cars are identified: Gatsby's Rolls-Royce (not his personal car), Nick's Dodge, and the Ford in Wilson's garage. Three celebrities are named: Joe Frisco, Gilda Grey, and David Belasco – all from show business. Two criminals – Charles Becker and Herman Rosenthal – are mentioned. Yet Fitzgerald's invented list of the attendees at Gatsby's party has become a source for students of Prohibition society. The laureate of the Jazz Age had little interest in jazz. His music was the popular songs of the era, six of which are mentioned in the novel: "The Sheik of Araby," "The Love Nest," "Ain't We Got Fun?" "Three O'Clock in the Morning," "The Rosary," and "Beale Street Blues" (a 1917 jazz work by W. C. Handy that was a popular dance tune).

Although he had a keen sense of history, Fitzgerald was indifferent to many of the causes and activities of the twenties. Despite his call for political and social change annexed to *This Side of Paradise* (1920), he soon abandoned that concern. He ignored the Sacco and Vanzetti case, which enlisted his literary friends. When Fitzgerald came to write his 1931 postmortum, "Echoes of the Jazz Age," he observed: "It was characteristic of the Jazz Age that it had no interest in politics at all."[19] This generalization doesn't hold, but it applies to Fitzgerald. His claim that he had been influenced by *The Decline of the West* – "I read him [Spengler] the same summer I was writing *The Great Gatsby* and I don't think I ever quite recovered from him"[20] – does not bear scrutiny. *The Decline of the West* was not available in English in the summer of 1924.

Another subject of general interest in the twenties that Fitzgerald was ignorant of was the stock market. Nevertheless, he was able to convey the Eldorado mood that provides the back-

---

†All quotations from *The Great Gatsby* in this volume are cited from the first printing (New York: Scribners, 1925) as emended in Matthew J. Bruccoli, *Apparatus for F. Scott Fitzgerald's The Great Gatsby* (Columbia: University of South Carolina Press, 1974).

ground for *The Great Gatsby*. Nick Carraway decides to enter the investment field because "Everybody I knew was in the bond business" (p. 3). When James B. ("Rot-Gut") Ferret left the gambling table at Gatsby's party, "it meant that he was cleaned out and Associated Traction would have to fluctuate profitably next day" (p. 75). Gatsby is involved with Meyer Wolfsheim in a securities swindle, as well as bootlegging, but Fitzgerald was unable to document this activity. When Maxwell Perkins read the unrevised typescript, he noted that Gatsby's criminal activities were vague. Fitzgerald admitted that the flaw resulted from his own ignorance: "But I know now – and as a penalty for not having known first, in other words make sure, I'm going to tell more."[21] Although Fitzgerald subsequently reported to Perkins that "I've accounted for his money,"[22] he only supplied clues that Gatsby was involved in illegal endeavors. His source was a man in Rome who briefed him on the 1922 Fuller–McGee Case, in which the partners in a brokerage firm were charged with misappropriating clients' funds. Arnold Rothstein, the remote source for Wolfsheim, the man who fixed the 1919 World Series, was implicated.

Writing to Corey Ford from Hollywood a dozen years after *The Great Gatsby*, Fitzgerald described his method of treating material:

> In *This Side of Paradise* (in a crude way) and in *Gatsby* I selected the stuff to fit a given mood or "hauntedness" or whatever you might call it, rejecting in advance in *Gatsby*, for instance, all the ordinary material for Long Island, big crooks, adultery theme and always starting from the *small* focal point that impressed me – my own meeting with Arnold Rothstein, for instance.[23]

Fitzgerald did not work directly from models; he did not attempt to copy life. He transmuted his impressions. "Whether it's something that happened twenty years ago or only yesterday, I must start out with an emotion – one that's close to me and that I can understand."[24]

The figure who controls Gatsby's mysterious wealth is a travesty of Rothstein. Fitzgerald attempted to document Wolfsheim's criminal background through his reminiscences of the 1912 Rosenthal–Becker murder case, but the facts are distorted to accommodate Wolfsheim's sentimentality. Except for the touch of menace provided by his human-molar cufflinks, Wolfsheim is a comic racketeer – as is Gatsby in different ways.‡ O'Hara, one of Fitzgerald's staunchest admirers, commented: "I fully believed Gatsby until I went to NY and met some of those mob people. Gatsby would not have lasted a week with the ones I met, let alone taken control."[25]

Despite inaccuracies and absurdities, *The Great Gatsby* has become a source for historians because of Fitzgerald's sense of time, of the emotions evoked by particular moments. In *This Side of Paradise* he formulated a distinction that he used twice in the novel: "the sentimental person thinks things will last – the romantic person has a desperate confidence that they won't."[26] Many writers have been distinguished by a sense of the past; Fitzgerald possessed a complex and delicate sense of the passing present. Malcolm Cowley has observed that Fitzgerald wrote as if surrounded by clocks and calendars.

Fitzgerald's primary concern was with the rhythms, the colors, the tones associated with time and place – often expressed through synesthesia, as in "yellow cocktail music" (p. 49). Time and place are inseparable in Fitzgerald: not just how it was, but how it felt in "a transitory enchanted moment" (p. 217). He later wrote, "After all, any given moment has its value; it can be questioned in the light of after-events, but the moment remains."[27] His task was to fix and preserve evanescent experience. Fitzgerald's sense of mood was extraordinary: the summer twilight in New York, the riotous Long Island nights, the Chicago railroad station at holiday time (yet he stipulated the wrong station before Ring Lardner corrected it). These passages have become touchstones of American prose.

At the end of "Echoes of the Jazz Age" he observed: "and it all seems rosy and romantic to us who were young then, because we will never feel quite as intensely about our surroundings any more."[28] This theme is not the same as the familiar *ubi sunt* for-

---

‡Bootlegger Max von Gerlach was a partial source for Gatsby. A quarter of a century after the novel was published, the fifty-five-year-old proprietor of a Flushing, Long Island, used-car business shot himself (*New York World-Telegram*, December 22, 1939, 4). See Matthew J. Bruccoli, " 'How Are You and the Family Old Sport?' - Gerlach and Gatsby," *Fitzgerald/Hemingway Annual 1975*, pp. 33–36.

mula. Fitzgerald and his heroes do not yearn for the melted snows of yesteryear; they mourn for their lost capacity to respond to those snows: "the snow of twenty-nine wasn't real snow. If you didn't want it to be snow, you just paid some money."[29]

The strongest feeling generated by *The Great Gatsby* is regret. It is not regret keyed to mutability – which means change. Fitzgerald evokes regret for depleted emotional capacity, a regret as intense as the emotions that inspired it were. While he was writing *The Great Gatsby*, Fitzgerald explained: "That's the whole burden of this novel – the loss of those illusions that give such color to the world that you don't care whether things are true or false as long as they partake of the magical glory."[30]

In "Winter Dreams," the 1922 story that is a miniature of *The Great Gatsby*, poor boy Dexter Green becomes wealthy but loses the rich girl who catalyzed his ambitions. This is his response to her home as published in the magazine text:

> There was a feeling of mystery in it, of bedrooms upstairs more beautiful and strange than other bedrooms, of gay and radiant activities taking place through these deep corridors and of romances that were not musty and laid already in lavender, but were fresh and breathing and set forth in rich motor cars and in great dances whose flowers were scarcely withered.[31]

When Fitzgerald rewrote this passage in Chapter 8 of the novel for Gatsby's response to Daisy Fay's home – scrupulously cutting it from the collected text of the story – "rich motor cars" became "this year's shining motor-cars" (p. 178). Not just expensive cars, but the cars that evoke the aura of a particular time.

At the end of "Winter Dreams," Green is told that the beauty of his dream girl has "faded."

> For the first time in years the tears were streaming down his face. But they were for himself now. He did not care about mouth and eyes and moving hands. He wanted to care but could not care. For he had gone away and he could never come back anymore. The gates were closed, the sun was gone down, and there was no beauty but the gay beauty of steel that withstands all time. Even the grief he could have borne was left behind in the country of illusion, of youth, of the richness of life, when his winter dreams had flourished.
>
> "Long ago," he said, "long ago, there was something in me, but

now that thing is gone. Now that thing is gone, that thing is gone. I
cannot cry. I cannot care. That thing will come back no more."[32]

Green grieves for his capacity to respond to "the richness of life,"
but he nonetheless yields to time and loss. Gatsby doesn't: " 'Can't
repeat the past?' he cried incredulously. 'Why of course you
can!' " (p. 133).

The Great Gatsby is time-haunted from "In my younger and
more vulnerable years" to "borne back ceaselessly into the past."
There are at least 450 time words in the novel.[33] Exclusive of
character names, the second most frequent noun is *time*, with 87
occurrences. (*House* appears 95 times.) *Moment* or *moments* occur
73 times; *day* or *days*, 70; *minute* or *minutes*, 49; *hour* or *hours*, 47;
o'clock, 26; *year*, 19; *past*, 18 (as against 5 appearances of *future*);
month or *months*, 15; *week* or *weeks*, 15; *twilight*, 9; *clock*, 6; *watch*
(noun), 5; *time-table*, 3. The first striking image in the novel is the
Buchanans' lawn "jumping over sun-dials" (p. 8).

In Chapter 5, the fulcrum of the nine-chapter novel, when
Gatsby is reunited with Daisy, his "head leaned back so far that it
rested against the face of a defunct mantlepiece clock" (p. 104). A
moment later Gatsby almost knocks the clock off the mantle,
"whereupon he turned and caught it with trembling fingers, and
set it back in place" (p. 105). The irony of this symbolism may be
too blatant. Gatsby, the time defier, rescues a defunct timepiece,
but time will put him "back in place." When Gatsby takes Daisy to
tour his house later in this chapter, Klipspringer plays the piano
and Fitzgerald provides the lyric:

> In the morning,
> In the evening,
> > Ain't we got fun –
>
> . . .
>
> In the meantime,
> In between time –

And when Daisy leaves Gatsby's party in the next chapter, the
orchestra is playing "Three O'Clock in the Morning" – "a neat,
sad little waltz of that year" (p. 131).

Fitzgerald's treatment of time with the effect of simultaneous
detachment and involvement – what Cowley described as "dou-

ble vision"[34] – reinforces the permeation of realism and imagination that identifies his best fiction. Thus, Nick jots down the names of the people who came to Gatsby's parties on a timetable headed "This schedule is in effect July 5th, 1922" (p. 73). Such horology fosters the impression of historical truth – which is not the same thing as straight history.

4

The ebullient author of *This Side of Paradise* proclaimed in 1920 that "An Author ought to write for the youth of his own generation, the critics of the next, and the schoolmasters of ever afterward."[35] Five years later he achieved those aims – and more. Now the young readers, the scholar-critics, and the schoolmasters are engaged with *Gatsby* and Gatsby. Yet no one in 1925 predicted the present eminence of *The Great Gatsby* – not even Fitzgerald.

The essays commissioned for this volume investigate several aspects of the stature of *The Great Gastby*. They provide answers to the question of why this short novel, which seemed to be dead before its author, rose from the graveyard of "dated" fiction and assumed its rightful position among the American masterpieces. Of course it is dated – as are all works of literature. Critics praise timeless works, but a timeless work is one that people keep reading.

The contributors have addressed those qualities of *Gatsby* that contribute to its staying power. Richard Anderson has gone back to Fitzgerald's 1920 statement and traced the evidence of the great *Gatsby* revival. Roger Lewis has examined *Gatsby*'s treatment of the suppressed American theme of money – in particular, the connection between love and money. Susan Resneck Parr has examined the role of illusion in establishing order within the world of the novel. Kenneth E. Eble has placed the novel in the tradition of America's quest for an American literature. George Garrett has approached it from the perspective of a novelist, responding to the miracles of Fitzgerald's style.

The Great Gatsby is inexhaustible. Thirty-five years after the resuscitation of the novel, it has been possible to assemble these useful new essays. It seems safe to forecast that, with or without the valuable work represented here, *The Great Gatsby* and deserving readers will always find each other. And the discovery must be a private act. After that happens, the serious reader will require the kind of help this collection provides.

NOTES

1 *Correspondence of F. Scott Fitzgerald*, ed. Matthew J. Bruccoli and Margaret M. Duggan (New York: Random House, 1980), p. 112.
2 Specimens of the revised galleys are included in *The Great Gatsby: A Facsimile of the Manuscript*, ed. Matthew J. Bruccoli (Washington, D.C.: Bruccoli Clark/Microcard, 1973).
3 *Dear Scott/Dear Max*, ed. Jackson Bryer and John Kuehl (New York: Scribners, 1971), p. 94.
4 "Spring Flight," *The Dial* 79 (August 1925):162–4.
5 "New York Chronicle," *New Criterion* 4 (January 1926):170–1.
6 "As H.L.M. Sees It," *Baltimore Evening Sun*, May 2, 1925, p. 9.
7 *The Saturday Review of Literature* (April 25, 1925), p. 709.
8 Ibid., p. 777.
9 *TLS*, February 18, 1926, p. 116; *London Mercury* 13 (April 1926):656–8; *New Criterion* 4 (October 1926):773–6; *Saturday Review*, February 20, 1926, pp. 234–5.
10 New York: Modern Library, 1934, p. x.
11 December 23, 1940, p. 19.
12 "Not Wholly Lost," December 24, 1940, p. 14.
13 December 24, 1940, p. 4.
14 January 4, 1941, p. 9.
15 "Fitzgerald and the Press," *The New Republic*, February 17, 1941, p. 213.
16 See Jackson R. Bryer and G. T. Tanselle, "*The Great Gatsby* – A Study in Literary Reputation," *New Mexico Quarterly* 33 (Winter 1963–4):409–25; also Bryer, *F. Scott Fitzgerald: The Critical Reception* (New York: Franklin, 1978).
17 William Troy, "Scott Fitzgerald – The Authority of Failure," *Accent* 6 (Autumn 1945):56–60; John Berryman, "F. Scott Fitzgerald," *Kenyon Review* 7 (Winter 1946):103–12.
18 John O'Hara, Introduction to *The Portable F. Scott Fitzgerald* (New York: Viking Press, 1945), p. xii.
19 *Scribner's Magazine* (November 1931):459–65. Reprinted in *The Crack-Up*.
20 "To Maxwell Perkins," *The Letters of F. Scott Fitzgerald*, ed. Andrew Turnbull (New York: Scribners, 1963), pp. 289–90.

21 Turnbull, ed., *Letters*, p. 173.

22 Ibid., p. 177.

23 Ibid., p. 551.

24 "One Hundred False Starts," *The Saturday Evening Post*, March 4, 1933, pp. 13, 65−6.

25 *Selected Letters of John O'Hara*, ed. Matthew J. Bruccoli (New York: Random House, 1978), p. 425.

26 New York: Scribners, 1920, p. 246.

27 "Six of One −," *Redbook* 58 (February 1932):22−5, 86, 88. Collected in *The Price Was High* (New York: Harcourt Brace Jovanovich/Bruccoli Clark, 1979).

28 See note 16.

29 "Babylon Revisited," *The Saturday Evening Post*, February 21, 1931, pp. 3−5, 82−4. Collected in *Taps at Reveille*.

30 To Ludlow Fowler, *Correspondence of F. Scott Fitzgerald*, ed. Matthew J. Bruccoli and Margaret Duggan (New York: Random House, 1980), p. 145.

31 *Metropolitan Magazine* 56 (December 1922):11−15, 98, 100−2, 104−7. Collected in *All the Sad Young Men*.

32 *All the Sad Young Men* (New York: Scribners, 1926), p. 90.

33 Andrew T. Crosland, *Concordance to The Great Gatsby* (Detroit: Gale Research, 1975).

34 "Fitzgerald: The Double Man," *Saturday Review of Literature*, February 24, 1951, pp. 9−10, 42−4.

35 "The Author's Apology," *This Side of Paradise*, third printing (New York: Scribners, 1920).

2

Gatsby's Long Shadow:
Influence and Endurance

RICHARD ANDERSON

IN his 1944 novel *The Lost Weekend*, Charles Jackson permits his protagonist, Don Birnam, to fall into the fantasy of lecturing to a literature class (the novel's time is roughly 1935):

> He took down *The Great Gatsby* and ran his finger over the fine green binding. "There's no such thing," he said aloud, "as a flawless novel. But if there is, this is it." He nodded. The class looked and listened in complete attention, and one or two made notes. . . . "People will be going back to Fitzgerald one day as they now go back to Henry James." He walked back and forth, tapping the book in his hand. "Pay no attention, either, to those who care for his writing merely; who speak of 'the texture of his prose' and other silly and borrowed and utterly meaningless phrases. True, the writing is the finest and purest, the most entertaining and most readable, that we have in America today . . . but it's the content that counts in literature. . . . Apart from his other gifts, Scott Fitzgerald has the one thing that a novelist needs: a truly seeing eye."[1]

In *Southern Women*, Lois Battle's novel published forty years after *The Lost Weekend*, four women discuss social relationships. They are going to a party in the Hamptons. Maxine speaks first:

> "There'll be a lot of new men at Mel's tonight. You know Mel always entertains as though he was the reincarnation of the Great Gatsby."
> "Mel's got style," Estelle agreed.
> "No. Mel's got money," Ginny said.
> "Will Mel have food?" Cordy said.
> "There'll be everything you want there," Maxine assured her. "Everything."
> Fifteen minutes later, as Maxine squeezed her car into a place between a BMW and a Rolls, Cordy saw that for once Maxine had not been exaggerating. Except for a twelve-foot satellite dish antenna sitting in the middle of the floodlit lawns, this really might have been the Gatsby estate.[2]

In several ways, these two passages from American novels published subsequent to the death of F. Scott Fitzgerald in 1940 frame his impact on American literature. They help measure the endurance of his writing, particularly *The Great Gatsby*, in the tradition of American fiction. First, they establish chronological outlines, more or less. From even before his death (if we accept the reality of Don Birnam's fictional "life") through the present, American novelists have used *Gatsby* as a literary peg. In so doing, they indicate the persistence of that novel as both a benchmark of quality and a popular literary landmark, a work any reader sufficiently literate to be enjoying the novels from which they come is presumed to know and appreciate. The two passages also stake out the polarities of *Gatsby*'s presence. Jackson's passionate, insistent tribute is that of a writer who recognizes in a predecessor magnitude of achievement – the application of craftsmanship in the service of sensibility that shapes the best art. Battle rather casually makes an allusive comparison that she knows will stimulate standard visions of grandeur, easily recognized by a wide spectrum of readers. Finally, the two passages help measure the growth of Fitzgerald's reputation, in particular as it depends upon the stature of *The Great Gatsby*, in the four and a half decades since his death. Jackson – the passionate disciple whose novel is permeated by the influence of Fitzgerald's style, tone, and moral vision – feels he must argue almost shrilly for the legitimacy of his mentor's achievement. Battle can take that achievement for granted, drawing naturally upon Fitzgerald rather like Fitzgerald and his contemporaries had drawn upon Shakespeare or Keats.

Measurement of literary permanence is a risky undertaking, especially when it involves a writer whose work has not yet stood a substantial test of time. Nevertheless, few scholars or readers would deny that, by the usual criteria, Fitzgerald's influence has made itself felt as strongly as has that of any American novelist. There are four main tests of Fitzgerald's and Gatsby's endurance: the ways the author and the novel have impressed themselves on the general public; sales figures; academic–scholarly activity, and – of special interest – the responses of other writers in their own work.

The first biography, Arthur Mizener's *The Far Side of Paradise*

(1951),[3] in conjunction with Budd Schulberg's novel *The Disenchanted* (1950)[4] — which recounted the last days in Hollywood of a burnt-out Jazz Age novelist — had the effect of establishing a popular image of Fitzgerald that has only in the past few years begun to be dispelled. Fitzgerald himself had contributed to this intensely romantic, nostalgic, and sentimental image of the brilliant young chronicler of the 1920s — daring, adventurous, but self-destructive, who became the saddened, emotionally bankrupt Hollywood writer struggling against alcohol, illness, and failure to achieve final self-respect and artistic success. His public interviews in the 1920s, his self-examining essays in the 1930s (such as the "Crack-up" series in *Esquire*), his tormented marriage, and his self-doubting correspondence, as they all began to find publication following his death, made good material for journalists and even for some men of letters and academics who wished to see him as the ruined poet of modern American letters. He was for them the "poor Scott Fitzgerald" who had, he wrote in "Pasting It Together," "*become identified with the objects of my horror or compassion.*"[5] This was a pitiable but noble Fitzgerald, who had sacrificed all for glamor and success, then watched it slide from his fingers while the nation had watched the bright lights of the twenties dim into the Depression. Warm compassion for Poor Scott was reinforced by the general wave of nostalgia for the Jazz Age that swept the United States in the 1950s. That nostalgia helped establish a popular awareness of Fitzgerald that had a life related to, but not dependent upon, his novels and stories. Fitzgerald the romantic figure, as opposed to Fitzgerald's work, was the subject matter of nonfiction books, thinly disguised novels, radio and television plays, and a film.

The popular image of Fitzgerald, something of a combination of the youthful Byron and the dying Keats, undoubtedly became fused, in many American consciousnesses, with images of his protagonists Amory Blaine, Jay Gatsby, and Dick Diver. How much this confusion reinforced Fitzgerald's literary reputation as a slipshod caretaker of an unfulfilled talent is difficult to assess. Ultimately, it may have led readers to the novels and stories themselves and thus may actually have worked to establish his merit rather than obscure it. Certainly, this public Fitzgerald has played some part in consolidating in the American consciousness the permanence of Gatsby: both the character Jay Gatsby, whose shadow falls across the face of modern American fiction as does that of no other figure from American literature, and the novel *The Great Gatsby*, which is admired, emulated, and used as a basis of reference and allusion to an extent only a few works – *Huckleberry Finn, The Waste Land*, arguably *Moby-Dick* – can claim. The fusion, at some level of the public mind, of F. Scott Fitzgerald and Jay Gatsby – mistaken and simplistic though it may be – has served to make Gatsby a figure of nostalgic mythologizing with power to stir imaginations that have never encountered the pages of the novel. America took Scott and Zelda Fitzgerald to its heart, following the first wave of the Fitzgerald revival culminating in *The Far Side of Paradise* and *The Disenchanted*. In the subsequent thirty-five years, as overall awareness and appreciation of Fitzgerald's fiction swelled, so did the appropriation into American literature of the images of the Fitzgeralds.

On the most superficial level, that appreciation has found expression in the countless "Scott Fitzgerald–look" clothing advertisements, or in the bars and nightclubs with names like "Zelda's" or "Gatsby's Place"; in less ephemeral and more dignified ways, the Fitzgeralds have come to be subject matter for American literature. *The Disenchanted* established a tradition much emulated. Schulberg denied identification between Fitzgerald and his novel's protagonist Manley Halliday; nevertheless, that identification was firmly established by the parallels between events in the book and those described in accounts of Fitzgerald's last years in Hollywood – especially after his companion Sheilah Graham published *Beloved Infidel*,[6] her 1958 memoir of her life with Fitzgerald during his last years. Not only did the two books find wide readership during the 1950s, but each carried the tragic romance of Fitzgerald to the public in other ways. *The Disenchanted* was dramatized for the stage, opening on Broadway in December 1957, and *Beloved Infidel* was made into a 1959 movie. The film was not successful, but Sheilah Graham claims that it spurred the making of the long-delayed David O. Selznick film of *Tender Is the Night*, released at the beginning of 1962.[7] The public identification of the principal characters with the Fitzgeralds – fallacious in part – nevertheless

strengthened the growing hold Fitzgerald and his work were ex-
erting on American culture.

Two teleplays of Fitzgerald's short story "The Last of the Belles"
are similar examples of the fusion of literary and biographical
appeal. The first was presented on the "Kraft Theatre" series in
1957;[8] the second appeared, with much advertising, as "F. Scott
Fitzgerald and 'The Last of the Belles,' " an American Broadcasting
Company (ABC) special presentation on January 7, 1974. The
deliberate biographical identification evident in the title of the
ABC version indicates an interest in Scott and Zelda Fitzgerald,
assumed to be models for characters in the story.

The dramatic interplay of the lives and careers of the Fitzgeralds
has had even more direct appeal to playwrights of the past decade.
Paul Hunter's off–Broadway play *Scott and Zelda* had a deliberately
brief run in January 1974, but it received favorable notices.[9] Much
more ambitious, if less successful, was *Clothes for a Summer Hotel*,
Tennessee Williams's exploration of the Fitzgeralds' lives, and the
interrelationship between life and art, which opened on Broadway
on March 26, 1980.[10] Subtitled *A Ghost Play*, it was less a tribute to
Ibsen than to Strindberg in its dreamlike fusion of time, place, and
character, as the Fitzgeralds recapitulated their lives within the
framework of Zelda Fitzgerald's asylum shortly before her death.
More recently, a local ballet troupe in Montgomery, Alabama,
birthplace of Zelda Fitzgerald, presented a ballet about her life,
using a memory framework structure similar to that of Williams's
play.

But it is in fiction itself that the image of F. Scott Fitzgerald, as
man and writer, has its most intriguing manifestations. As might
be expected, his presence appeared earliest in works written by his
contemporaries, particularly those on the Scribners list. His friend,
rival, and literary touchstone Ernest Hemingway incorporated him
by name, almost as a kind of taunting joke, into his 1936 short
story "The Snows of Kilimanjaro" as an example of a once effective writer ruined by his fascination with the romance of money.
The invented exchange between "Poor Scott Fitzgerald," the wor-
shipper of the rich, and Hemingway the realist (they have more
money) has become one of the best-known anecdotes in modern

American literary lore.[11] Hemingway's treatment of both Scott and Zelda Fitzgerald in his 1964 memoir–history *A Moveable Feast*[12] is sufficiently dramatic and creative that, although assuredly based on fact, his characterization might be termed fictive in its power and in the part it played in shaping the myth of Fitzgerald during the 1960s. The character Hunt Conroy in Thomas Wolfe's *The Web and the Rock* (1939) is also a fictional depiction of Fitzgerald.

More recently, as thinly disguised roman à clef characters, the Fitzgeralds appeared in George Zuckerman's 1969 novel *The Last Flapper*.[13] An exploitation of the legend of Zelda Fitzgerald's life (with an F. Scott Fitzgerald character in the background), the novel betrays its flavor in the paperback cover blurb: "They were young, rich, successful, happy, and had a mad whirl through the wild, crazy, drunken 20s. It was a path that could only lead to destruction. . . . Rannah O'Donell, beautiful and damned: The Last Flapper." In James Aldridge's *One Last Glimpse* (1977),[14] Fitzgerald appears directly as a character, observed during a fictional 1929 automobile trip with Ernest Hemingway. Aldridge's framework allowed him to explore the personal and professional relationships and tensions between the two. His narrative technique, focused through a young companion–narrator, was evidence of his admiration for Fitzgerald's structure in *Gatsby*.[15]

Whereas much of the material previously described reflects, with varying degrees of literary value, a fascination with the lives and legend of the Fitzgeralds, American fiction of the 1950s and 1960s also began to reflect deep admiration for the author of *The Great Gatsby* as a literary craftsman. Writers as varied as John Cheever, J. P. Marquand, Jack Kerouac, Vance Bourjaily, Raymond Chandler, and especially John O'Hara were admirers of Fitzgerald's mastery of style, image, and subject matter – sufficiently so that their admiration appeared in their writing. Cheever's tribute took the form of a contribution on Fitzgerald to the volume *Atlantic Brief Lives*, a compilation of biographical sketches of artists and writers. In illustrating Fitzgerald's literary excellence, Cheever quoted Nick Carraway's description of returning home to the Midwest from school in the East and emphasized Fitzgerald's profound immersion in his time as the mark of a great writer: "In Fitzgerald there is a thrilling sense of knowing exactly where one is – the city, the resort, the hotel, the decade and the time of day. His greatest innovation was to use social custom, clothing, overheard music, not as history but as an expression of his acute awareness of the meaning of his time."[16] As has been pointed out elsewhere, John P. Marquand was also an admirer of Fitzgerald. His 1930 novel *Warning Hill* has Fitzgeraldian qualities, including an allusion to Fitzgerald's short story "The Rich Boy" (1926).[17]

One group of American writers who have a surprising affinity for Fitzgerald are those who seriously practice the craft of mystery writing, using the "hard-boiled detective" genre. One of the fore-most of them, Raymond Chandler, was an admirer of Fitzgerald's craftsmanship. In a 1950 letter Chandler described Fitzgerald's literary distinction as "one of the rarest qualities in all literature," a kind of "charm – charm as Keats would have used it. . . . It's not a matter of pretty writing or clear style. It's a kind of subdued magic, controlled and exquisite, the sort of thing you get from good string quartets. Yes, where would you find it today?"[18] A few years later, drawing another analogy to romantic poetry, Chandler alluded to Fitzgerald in *The Long Goodbye:* a farewell note from a man detective Philip Marlowe has been tracing is signed "Roger (F. Scott Fitzgerald) Wade." The man's wife tells Marlowe that her husband had been a great admirer of Fitzgerald, describing him as the "best drunken writer since Coleridge, who took dope."[19]

Jack Kerouac, quintessential 1950s Beat Generation social rebel, would seem an unlikely disciple of Fitzgerald's work, but his 1959 picaresque work *Doctor Sax* bears this tribute:

> It was a funny song, at the end it had that 1930's lilt so hysterical
> Scott Fitzgerald, with writhely women squirmelying their we-a-ares
> in silk & brocade shiny New Year's Eve nightclub dresses with
> thrown champagne and popples busting "Gluyr! the New Year's
> Parade!"[20]

Even in his identification of Fitzgerald with a bourgeois value system he was rejecting, Kerouac displayed a fasciantion with the romantic freedom Fitzgerald and his work represented to many younger writers. In a 1962 *Life* magazine tribute to a preparatory school classmate, Kerouac wrote: "Nobody'll ever know America completely because nobody ever knew Gatsby, I guess."[21]

A more substantial and eloquent tribute was the 1964 story by Vance Bourjaily, "Fitzgerald Attends My Fitzgerald Seminar,"[22] which concerns the efforts of a professor of English to interest cynical 1960-ish graduate students in the mood and style of the stories in *Flappers and Philosophers,* while imagining that Fitzgerald himself is looking on. The extent of Professor Short's (and, by extension, Bourjaily's) admiration for Fitzgerald's work is evident, and the story demonstrates that, by 1964, awareness of Fitzgerald's writings among young Americans went considerably beyond familiarity with one or two novels.

It is on the mind and heart of John O'Hara, however, that Fitzgerald made one of his strongest literary impressions and found one of his most vigorous champions. O'Hara had come of age under the influence of Fitzgerald's work during Fitzgerald's lifetime, and he had figured early and eloquently in the revival of Fitzgerald's reputation in the 1940s. From the very first, he insisted, Fitzgerald had had a shaping influence on his work. When his 1934 first novel, *Appointment in Samarra,* was republished in 1953,[23] O'Hara wrote a foreword in which he avowed that novel's indebtedness to Fitzgerald and voiced again the fervent championing of Fitzgerald's writing that had characterized such earlier comments as his 1941 *New Republic* essay "Certain Aspects" and his introduction to *The Portable F. Scott Fitzgerald* (1945). In the latter he had declared: "All he was was our best novelist, one of our best novella-ists, and one of our finest writers of short stories."[24] The elegiac tone of *Samarra,* its respect for detail and event as keys to character and meaning, and its reflection of just how people really talk and act are all marks of Fitzgerald's mature writing, qualities that would continue to appear throughout O'Hara's work. In the 1961 short story "Mrs. Stratton of Oak Knoll,"[25] O'Hara was more specific, permitting a character to make a ringing defense of Fitzgerald's art – as distinct from the superficiality of the John Held, Jr., caricatures with which the popular mind too often identified it.

If Fitzgerald in general, in the popular imagination and in his overall literary achievement, looms large in contemporary American culture, *The Great Gatsby* in particular has become so much a fact of American literature — so much a permanent presence, a persistent influence — that it is almost impossible to imagine contemporary American fiction without Jay Gatsby. No other figure in our literature has become so eponymous.

As with the more general images of the Fitzgeralds and Fitzgerald's work in American culture, the presence of Jay Gatsby can be measured in a number of ways, some superficial, others profound. Gatsby and the novel in which he lives have become firmly fixed in popular culture, in academic evaluation of literary achievement, and — perhaps most telling and most important — in the literature of other writers.

That ubiquitous presence is in part evidence of and concomitant with the popular image of Fitzgerald as writer, growing from and reflecting the widening outer circle of the Fitzgerald revival. If F. Scott Fitzgerald is, at some level of popular consciousness, America's Chatterton or Keats, Jay Gatsby is his character most closely identified with both the glamor and loss of his romance. As such, Gatsby, and *The Great Gatsby*, again and again come to public attention in ways not necessarily dependent on having read the novel. They can be as ephemeral as advertisements and commercial exploitation: In 1964, for instance, an ad for the Plaza Hotel in New York, setting for the confrontation scene between Gatsby and Tom Buchanan, incorporated a passage from the novel. In 1968, the Eagle Shirt company marketed a Great Gatsby shirt, available in an appropriately rich array of hues, including West Egg Blue.[26] In conjunction with the release in 1974 of the Paramount film of *Gatsby*, there was a veritable flood of Gatsby products, ranging from phonograph recordings of 1920s music to Gatsby sportswear by McGregor, coiffures by Glemby Hair Salons, Teflon II Cookwear, and Ballentine's Whisky.[27]

A more serious measure of the impact of *The Great Gatsby* can be achieved by looking at the number and kinds of literary collections, anthologies, and studies of American fiction that have included excerpts from the novel as examples of good fiction. Fitzgerald's bibliographer lists twelve that appeared between 1935 and 1977: *The Great American Parade* (1935), *North, East, South, West* (1945), *I Wish I'd Written That* (1946), *Taken at the Flood* (1946), *Better Reading II: Literature* (1948), *These Would I Choose*

(1948), *The Art of Book Reading* (1952), *The American Treasury 1455–1955* (1955), *An Anthology of American Humor* (1962), *Advanced Spanish Composition* (1971), *In the Presence of This Continent* (1971), and *The Saturday Evening Post Automobile Book* (1977).[28] The nature of the use of excerpts from the novel may be surmised from the titles of most of these, but a closer look at some representative volumes from the list provides a sense of the values editors and compilers saw in Fitzgerald's prose. *The Great American Parade*,[29] for example, sought to present a variety of ways in which "leading modern authors" had written about American people and places. As "The Guy Who Fixed the World Series," it incorporated Nick Carraway's account of his meeting Gatsby in Manhattan for lunch and his being introduced to Meyer Wolfshiem. In contrast to this interest in character depiction, Clifton Fadiman and Charles Van Doren chose for *The American Treasury 1455–1955*[30] two brief passages intended to illustrate Fitzgerald's command of imagery and symbol: one a description of caterwauling automobile horns after one of Gatsby's parties, the other the closing paragraphs, from Gatsby's belief in the green light through the eloquent cadences describing humanity as beating against the currents of time. This anthology also incorporated passages from other Fitzgerald works. *The Art of Book Reading*,[31] an instructional text, used the selection describing the death of Gatsby in his swimming pool to illustrate how to read effectively at the climax of a novel. Most eloquent as a tribute, however, was *I Wish I'd Written That*, a collection of passages chosen by famous American Authors from works they admired.[32] For it, John Dos Passos, Fitzgerald's friend and contemporary who had been one of the champions of his reputation in the years following his death, chose the evocative description of the wasteland/ash heap lying between West Egg and Astoria, the "Valley of Ashes."

If the drama of *Gatsby* has touched anthologists, it is not at all surprising that it has enthralled those involved with the American stage and screen. Productions have ranged from a 1956 musical adapted from the novel by the Yale Dramatic Association with book and lyrics by Aubrey Goodman,[33] through a 1957 Playhouse 90 television adaptation,[34] to the 1984 Broadway production of A. R. Gurney, Jr.'s, *The Golden Age*. The plot of the last, loosely based on Henry James's *The Aspern Papers* focuses on missing chapters from *The Great Gatsby*. Hollywood film versions of the novel have also both contributed to and manifested the presence of Gatsby in the national consciousness. There have been three productions, beginning with the silent version in 1927 with Warner Baxter as Gatsby, continuing with the 1949 Alan Ladd Gatsby, to the 1974 Robert Redford impersonation.

It may be useful to address briefly the relationship among the realms of publishing, scholarship, and literary fiction during the 1960s and 1970s – when Fitzgerald's reputation was being consolidated and *Gatsby* was being thrust, in a number of ways, upon the reading public.

During the 1940s, Scribners permitted other houses to publish Fitzgerald's works, probably as a way of testing the legitimacy of the Fitzgerald revival.[35] *Gatsby* was the most frequently reprinted novel. By 1951 the revival was well established, and Scribners assumed control of the canon. At first, Scribners combined *Gatsby* with other works, as in its 1953 *Modern Standard Authors: Three Novels of F. Scott Fitzgerald*, allowing Penguin to reprint *Gatsby* in Britain. In 1958, a separate Scribners *Gatsby* trade edition was reissued. At the same time, a new readership was being explored: The combination of paperbound technology and the growth of school-age readers during the post–World War II baby boom led Scribners to concentrate on reprints aimed at students. In 1957, a Student's Edition was published. It was so successful that in 1960 it became the first volume in the Scribner Library series of quality paperback reprints aimed primarily at high school and college readers. In 1961, a School Edition, with guiding material aimed at high school students, appeared. The next years saw *Gatsby* included in *The Fitzgerald Reader* (1963), edited by Arthur Mizener, and the *Quarto of Modern Literature* (1964), edited by Malcolm Cowley, long a Fitzgerald supporter. (He had contributed to the consolidation of Fitzgerald's reputation by editing both a revised *Tender Is the Night* and the *Stories*, including some previously uncollected, in the early 1950s.) In 1968 there was a large-type edition, and in 1970 a critical anthology incorporating *Gatsby* with research material, edited by Henry Dan Piper. That same year saw the distribution of a book club edition as part of a set issued by the

Literary Guild. In 1974, in conjunction with the Paramount film, Scribners permitted Bantam to publish an inexpensive paperback.

Throughout the period, Penguin continued to keep *Gatsby* available in Britain and abroad, issuing fourteen printings of its edition between 1950 and 1970. In 1948, Grey Walls Press had published a hardbound edition in England, which had modest sales through two printings. In 1958, perhaps encouraged by the success of the Penguins, The Bodley Head led off the first volume of its multi-volume collected works of Fitzgerald with *Gatsby*, together with *The Last Tycoon*, selected stories, and an introduction by J. B. Priestly. *The Great Gatsby* with notes was published by Bodley Head in 1967. The sales represented by the various Scribners versions climbed steadily, if at first slowly, averaging a few thousand volumes a year in the early 1950s. With the discovery of the college paperback market, however, Scribners' sales of *Gatsby* began to rise rapidly: in 1957, 12,000; the next year, three times as many; by 1960, 100,000 or more a year; by the end of that decade, more than 300,000 volumes annually, a level that has been maintained. By 1974 Fitzgerald's publishers could proudly assert that his works were required reading in more than 2,400 American college and university courses.

It is not clear to what degree each is cause or effect, but the rapid growth of readership of *Gatsby* was accompanied by an equivalent explosion of critical and scholarly commentary and analysis. Perhaps students read *Gatsby* because their teachers were investigating its literary merits; perhaps professors were drawn toward analysis because they wished to teach a book their students – and the general public – were beginning to recognize as an American classic. Probably each activity stimulated the other. Certainly the growth of both was concomitant.

The Modern Language Association International Bibliography has for the past two decades consistently shown Fitzgerald's work to be among that of American authors most frequently examined, critiqued, and analyzed. In 1980 there were forty-two entries; in 1981, twenty-four; and in 1982, the most recent compilation, forty. Of those items (some of them in foreign publications, some in books or graduate research works, but the majority essays or articles in American quarterlies and journals), twenty-eight, or almost one-third, were written in part or totally on *The Great Gatsby*. Only a few writers, notably Mark Twain and William Faulkner, receive more attention.

Between 1940 and 1950, perhaps fifteen articles on Fitzgerald that might be termed academic or scholarly were published.[36] Many of them came from the pens of a few men, early associated with the Fitzgerald revival – Malcolm Cowley, Lionel Trilling, Arthur Mizener. In the next decade, approximately sixty scholarly or critical articles, excluding notes or queries, treated Fitzgerald's work wholly or substantially. Of these, twenty-eight, nearly half, were concerned primarily with *Gatsby*. Between 1960 and 1968, approximately eighty articles or notes on Fitzgerald appeared, many of them in the *Fitzgerald Newsletter*. Again, nearly half (thirty-four) dealt wholly or significantly with *The Great Gatsby*. By 1970, the consolidation of Fitzgerald's academic reputation was completed, but scholarly interest did not slacken.

The first biography of Fitzgerald appeared in 1951. There have been three more, as well as one of Zelda Sayre Fitzgerald, which concentrated on her relationship with her husband, and one that might be termed a study of both husband and wife. In 1957, the first nonbiographical book-length study of Fitzgerald appeared, James E. Miller's *The Fictional Technique of F. Scott Fitzgerald* (The Hague: Nijhoff). By 1974, ten others had been published, as well as at least five collections of critical essays. Between 1969 and 1979, the *Fitzgerald/Hemingway Annual*, under the editorship of Matthew J. Bruccoli, served as a focus for commentary, notes, and critical attention. Books of bibliographical, biographical, and critical focus continue to appear, some of them directed partly or entirely toward understanding or evaluating *The Great Gatsby*.

Inevitably, only some of this critical attention has been of lasting importance and insight. But because it helped focus attention upon the qualities that have made the novel worthy of acclaim as an artistic masterpiece, that criticism stimulated cultural permanence for *Gatsby* – and helps to account for it. Much of the broader critical attention useful in defining Jay Gatsby came early, in articles subsequently reprinted in widely available critical collections. Together, those articles helped delineate the major impact of *Gatsby* on the American consciousness. Essentially, the essays fall into three groups: those that explore technique and craftsmanship, those that attempt to identify the symbolic power of Gatsby as a mythic figure, and those that insist that the novel's greatest strength lies in its moral questioning of America's involvement with the magic and power of wealth.[37]

Of the first category, particularly effective as well as representative were John W. Bicknell's "The Waste Land of F. Scott Fitzgerald," *Virginia Quarterly Review* (Autumn 1954); Cleanth Brooks's "The American 'Innocence': In James, Fitzgerald, and Faulkner," *Shenandoah* (Autumn 1964); and Robert E. Long's two-part study *"The Great Gatsby* and the tradition of Joseph Conrad," *Texas Studies in Literature and Language* (Summer–Fall 1966) – all of which examined Fitzgerald's relationship with other major writers not primarily as influence studies, but as approaches in delineating craftsmanship. More extensive studies that have helped show Fitzgerald as a careful master of style, image, structure, and literary form in *Gatsby* include Kenneth E. Eble's *F. Scott Fitzgerald* (New York: Twayne, 1963), as well as Eble's valuable essay "The Craft of Revision: *The Great Gatsby,"* *American Literature* (November 1964); Robert Sklar's *F. Scott Fitzgerald: The Last Laocoön* (New York: Oxford University Press, 1967), with its careful analysis of the narrative technique provided through Nick Carraway; and two textual studies by Bruccoli: *The Great Gatsby: A Facsimile of the Manuscript* (Washington, DC: Bruccoli Clark/Microcard Editions, 1973) and *Apparatus for F. Scott Fitzgerald's The Great Gatsby* (Columbia: University of South Carolina Press, 1974).

The Great Gatsby came into critical favor at the height of the practice of the New Criticism, one emphasis of which was close readings of symbol and theme. It is not surprising that some of its best commentary was directed toward exploring the nature of Jay Gatsby as an embodiment of mythic and symbolic meaning. Some of that criticism – notably Robert W. Stallman's "Gatsby and the Hole in Time," *Modern Fiction Studies* (November 1955), and John Henry Raleigh's "Fitzgerald's *The Great Gatsby,"* *University of Kansas City Review* (June 1957) – place the novel in a universal mythic mode. Others – notably Floyd C. Watkins's "Fitzgerald's Jay Gatz and Young Ben Franklin," *The New England Quarterly* (June 1954); Robert Ornstein's "Scott Fitzgerald's Fable of East and

West,'' *College English* (December 1956); and especially Marius Bewley's treatment of Gatsby as a universal mythic hero, in *The Eccentric Design: Form in the Classic American Novel* (New York: Columbia University Press, 1959) — helped formulate a sense of Gatsby as a kinsman of major American mythic figures, from Benjamin Franklin through Huckleberry Finn. The theme of the relevance of the American dream to contemporary life, as enunciated in *Gatsby*, also received substantial examination in *The Eccentric Design* and in Milton R. Stern's *The Golden Moment* (Urbana: University of Illinois Press, 1970).

Another measure of the extent of Fitzgerald scholarship is the number of American Ph.D. dissertations written principally or wholly about Fitzgerald's work. The first one was completed in 1950. By 1982, seventy-four had been written.[38]

From this academic and scholarly activity can be drawn two conclusions that have a bearing on *The Great Gatsby*'s impact. First, combined with the publishing and sales history of the novel, the scholarship is clear evidence that articulate, educated readers coming of age in the past thrity years have had every opportunity to read and study *The Great Gatsby*. Second, the basic themes and concerns explored in the scholarship are those that have helped *Gatsby* captivate the American imagination: an extraordinary mastery of style, technique, image, and diction; a clear and detailed command of the nuances of the American fascination with success — not crass material riches but fulfillment measured by realizing a dream; a romantic purity undefiled by Jay Gatsby's limitations when that dream turns to dust; and a sense of national mythos involved in a figure both pioneer and gentleman, both commoner and natural nobleman.

The degree to which academic judgment of a literary reputation influences either popular opinion or that of other working writers is a question not easily answered. Probably the influence flows both ways, although, as Professor Jay B. Hubbell observed in *Who Are the Major American Writers?*,[39] in the United States authors of merit have frequently — in fact, usually — been recognized and appreciated by their fellow writers well before being accepted by the academic and critical establishment. Much the most important measure of the permanence and impact of a work of literature upon its culture is the impression it has made upon later writers working within the same cultural tradition. Certainly, by that measure, *The Great Gatsby* has left its mark more deeply than any other novel of its century. Both in the number of writers touched by it and in the quality of some of the works that openly or tacitly acknowledge discipleship, the scope of *Gatsby*'s profound effect can be gauged. *The Great Gatsby* may be the only novel in American literature that, in the variety and number of its emulators, has spawned a subliterature all its own: the *Gatsby* novels.

Certainly, the widespread use of *The Great Gatsby* in university classrooms helped bring the novel to the attention of millions of young Americans of the 1960s, 1970s, and 1980s, including some who would become writers of post–Fitzgerald literature; certainly, too, these younger writers were influenced by the critical interpretations and theories to which their teachers introduced them. To many writers of the postmodernist period, the grace, mythic scope, and moral earnestness of *The Great Gatsby* offered a pattern not always evident in much of their contemporary art. Perhaps Gatsby's insistence that innocence is recapturable, that the edenic past *can* be remade, appealed to a time hungry for beauty, ideals, and a sense of connectedness with fundamental American traditions.

To be sure, the shadow of Gatsby had begun to spread over American fiction before the baby boom generation came of age. As indicated earlier, a first manifestation was in *The Lost Weekend.* That novel's subject matter and theme – the abject failure of personality because of early inability to realize youthful romantic dreams, culminating in alcoholism – bear some resemblance to the popular image of Fitzgerald's life, as it was perceived in the 1940s. A more widely known tribute to *The Great Gatsby* is expressed by Holden Caulfield, the urban Huckleberry Finn of J. D. Salinger's *The Catcher in the Rye.* Holden himself has become one of the most enduring and endearing figures of American fiction, threading his way through the streets and the neuroses of modern America, as well as through – according to a recent paperback copy – thirty hardbound and eight-two paperback printings. A symbol of alienated youth to the young readers of the 1950s, Holden has come to be placed in a more romantic line of descent linking him to Mark Twain's Huck. That Jay Gatsby is also of that lineage, in Salinger's eyes, is evidenced by Holden's comments on the literary tastes his brother is attempting to develop in him:

> I still don't see how he could like a phony book like [Hemingway's *A Farewell to Arms*] and still like that one by Ring Lardner or that other one he's so crazy about, *The Great Gatsby*. . . . I was crazy about *The Great Gatsby*. Old Gatsby. Old sport. That killed me.[40]

That Holden was speaking for Salinger as well as for himself in his admiration for the (surprisingly) unphony Gatsby is reinforced by Gatsby-esque qualities in *Catcher:* a theme of revolt against the corruption of American innocence and a protagonist whose dreams are shattered by reality. Salinger's admiration was further expressed in a letter to a friend: "Re-read a lot of Scott Fitzgerald's work this week. God, I love that man. Damn fool critics are forever calling writers geniuses for their idiosyncracies [*sic*] — Hemingway for his reticent dialogue, Wolfe for his gargantuan energy, and so on. Fitzgerald's only idiosyncrasy was his pure brilliance."[41]

Less impresive, perhaps, but no less useful as evidence of the novel's persistence in the consciousnesses of American writers are tributes to *The Great Gatsby* that appeared in a scattering of novels of varied success over the decade after *Catcher*. In *The Boy Who Made Good* (1955), Mary Deasy's admiration for the biographical saga of Scott and Zelda Fitzgerald, as well as for the structure and tone of *Gatsby*, was abundantly evident. There is a first-person narrator—observer and the use of displaced chronology and with-held information. The emulation of *Gatsby* is unmistakable in the opening paragraph:

> The fall I went East to college for my freshman year, my father made a remark to me that I have never forgotten since.
> "Never let it bother you," he said, "if other people seem to get all the glory in life. Remember it's not always the kid everybody is watching who gets the brass ring and the free ride on the merry-go-round."[42]

In 1959, Aubrey Goodman, who had adapted *The Great Gatsby* for a musical at Yale in 1956, published *The Golden Youth of Lee Prince*, which has been described as reminiscent of Fitzgerald's novel.[43] The next year saw the publication of a much more widely read and well-received novel showing the influence of *Gatsby*: John O'Hara's *Ourselves to Know*.[44] Its structure echoes *Gatsby* in that it is narrated by an interested if skeptical investigator – in this instance a naive youth, Gerald Higgins, whose fascination with the shadowy figure of Robert Millhouser emulates (but not in exact parallel) Carraway's interest in Jay Gatsby. Higgins discovers early that Millhouser has, in the past, killed his wife. As Higgins comes to know Millhouser and – growing up – to undertake a biographical exploration, he learns that, as with Gatsby, appearances deceive, and the effort to understand is a process of growth.

The mid-sixties saw absorption of *The Great Gatsby* into the work of another master of the hard-boiled detective novel (*Gatsby* is, after all, a novel of mystery, as laced with realism as it is with poetry). The enthusiasm for Fitzgerald's work expressed by Kenneth Millar, who wrote as Ross Macdonald, was even less qualified than that of his predecessor and influence, Raymond Chandler. To the admiration Chandler had for Fitzgerald's style, Millar – a Ph.D. in English who had written his dissertation on Coleridge – brought an ear finely tuned to the lyricism and romance of *Gatsby*. In his Notebooks, he termed Fitzgerald:

> the last writer to embody the national fate, the last who swallowed whole the vast Platonic hubris of the Romantics, (Gatsby is said to have "drunk the Platonic milk of wonder"), the last who saw himself as a kind of dizzy philosopher–king at the apex of society, the last who projected his subjective life in fiction as a kind of tragic legend for his age and for future time.[45]

As early as 1958, Millar had told a newspaper interviewer that he greatly admired *Gatsby* and frequently reread it, calling the novel " 'the closest thing we have to a tragedy illustrating our secret history.' "[46] In *Black Money* (1965),[47] Millar put his admiration for *Gatsby* most clearly into his own work. In it Lew Archer, his private detective, investigates a mysterious and possibly criminal young man who has married a beautiful and sophisticated girl from a background of money and privilege. These elements of the romance between Gatsby and Daisy Fay are loosely adapted, but as Archer probes more and more deeply into the background of

"Francis Martel," alias "Feliz Cervantes," the sense of layer upon layer of partly true, partly false identity echoes the experience of Nick Carraway, who found that Gatsby had indeed been an "Oggsford man" and a war hero. Archer ultimately establishes that, like Jimmy Gatz, Martel-Cervantes is really a poor boy, Pedro Domingo from Panama, who had fallen in love with a golden princess, worked mightily to refine and better himself by a combination of means both admirable and corrupt, and run afoul of his erstwhile benefactor, a Nevada gambler–gangster who combines aspects of Dan Cody and Wolfshiem. Martel's golden girl proves as faithless as Daisy. Perhaps the most important resonance of *The Great Gatsby* in *Black Money*, though, is a thematic one: the effect of money, both on those who have it and those who, for whatever reasons, want it.

Later in the decade, another established novelist with a sense of social exactitude, Louis Auchincloss, paid his respects to *The Great Gatsby* in *A World of Profit* (1968).[48] Auchincloss traces the struggle of a poor boy to win a place in the glamorous world of wealth, as represented by a Long Island mansion. Like O'Hara, Auchincloss shares a technical affinity for careful observation of social behavior with the Fitzgerald of *Gatsby*. In an essay entitled *Three "Perfect Novels": And What They Have In Common*, Auchincloss cited *Gatsby* along with *The Scarlet Letter* and *Wuthering Heights*.[49]

The permanent impression *The Great Gatsby* has made on American fiction, as might be expected, is more direct and pronounced in the novels of writers who came of age during the 1950s and 1960s. C. D. B. Bryan's *The Great Dethriffe* (1970) was deliberately developed under the influence of the tone and mood of *Gatsby* and the aura of the Fitzgerald legend. Bryan, stepson of John O'Hara, created characters who are conscious of similarities between their 1950s and the 1920s, and they cultivate those parallels in an effort to create a *Gatsby* mood and tone in their own lives, as Bryan was doing in his novel. Like Fitzgerald, Bryan concentrated on capturing the mood of his times as his sensibility perceived and modified it. The lyrical quality of his prose and the use of a narrator–observer who develops into a central character bespeak the profound influence of Fitzgerald's novel on Bryan's, an influence directly voiced in several passages such as this one, contrasting the "real" F. Scott Fitzgerald of the 1930s with an earlier one:

> And then there is the mythical Fitzgerald: the golden distillation of Antibes twilights, of travelling home from schools in curtained Pullman sleeping cars, of champagne and hip flasks . . . a Fitzgerald who is forever more Gatsby than Carraway, whose shirts were not simply Brooks Brothers button-down whites, but rather like Gatsby's . . . shirts whose optimism Daisy Buchanan and an entire generation of her daughters might cry over. This was my Fitzgerald.[50]

The kind of brief allusion that indicates the widespread awareness of *The Great Gatsby* occurs in *Marion's Wall* (1973) by Jack Finney.[51] In a novel about the ghost of a 1920s film starlet, Finney incorporated the discovery of a long-lost print (fictional) of a silent film of *Gatsby*, directed by Ernst Lubitsch, and starring Rudolph Valentino as Gatsby, Gloria Swanson as Daisy, Greta Garbo as Jordan Baker, John Gilbert as Carraway, and Mae West, George O'Brien, and Harry Landon in supporting parts. In one of its party scenes appear Gilda Gray, Charles Chaplin and – best of all fantasies – Fitzgerald himself.

Ron Carlson's *Betrayed by F. Scott Fitzgerald* (1977) approached the image of Fitzgerald in general, and *Gatsby* in particular, from a different generational perspective: that of the Vietnam-era novel of black-humor protest. Carlson's narrator–protagonist, Larry Boosinger, undergoes a picaresque sequence of adventures occasioned by an impossibly romantic sensibility developed under the sway of Fitzgerald's literature. Neither the style nor the theme is directly patterned on *The Great Gatsby*, but from time to time a passage pays faintly (and fondly) mocking tribute, as in the opening paragraph: " 'Blame is not important,' my father used to say. 'Whose fault it is will not get anything fixed.' "[52] Most Gatsbyesque is the general theme that Larry finds the world well lost for his ideals.

A recent detective novelist placed in the hard-boiled tradition of Raymond Chandler and Ross Macdonald is Robert B. Parker. In *A Savage Place* (1981), detective Spenser seeks something to read: "I stopped at a drugstore on La Brea near Melrose and bought a copy of *The Great Gatsby* off the paperback rack. I hadn't read it in five years, and it was time again." A few hours (and pages) later, Spenser sums up his impression of Los Angeles as "a sunny buffoon of a city; corny and ornate and disorganized but kind of fun. The last hallucination, the dwindled fragment of − what had Fitzgerald called it? − 'the last and greatest of all human dreams.' "[53]

In that same year, 1981, appeared John Irving's widely read picaresque tragicomedy *The Hotel New Hampshire*.[54] More profoundly than any serious novel since O'Hara's *Ourselves to Know*, it bears the mark of *The Great Gatsby*. Most directly, it contains references to *Gatsby* by a minor character, Fraulein Fehlgeburt, a student of American literature at the University of Vienna. She is a strong admirer of *Gatsby*, to which she introduces the narrator–protagonist John Berry and his brother and sisters, one of whom, Lilly, is led to become a novelist by the power and beauty of Fitzgerald's novel. Fehlgeburt enunciates a theory of American literature as essentially romantic, with hints of a certain tragic suffering buried beneath the glamor of the romance. The Berrys, particularly Lilly, find the final passage of *Gatsby*, with its haunting images of fresh, innocent promise lost in the ceaseless current of time, so powerful that it haunts them. Lilly writes a successful first novel, but then struggles despairingly with her own impossible expectations, measured against the perfection of the ending of *Gatsby*, to continue her career. Unable to match Fitzgerald, who by implication has set an impossible standard for American prose fiction, she commits suicide in Manhattan, not far from the Plaza, where Gatsby and Tom Buchanan had their showdown.

The *Gatsby* references come late in the novel; only in retrospect is the reader likely to perceive less direct tributes and thematic resonances in *The Hotel New Hampshire*. Thematically, the novel traces the awful consequences of unbridled, innocent optimism, embodied in the quest of Win Berry, the clan's father, to establish a glamorous resort hotel such as the one in which he worked as a young man and where he met his wife. A wry, inverted Gatsby allusion is established early, in the glamor with which Win Berry invests his memory of the hotel's owner, a mysterious man in a white dinner jacket, who appears occasionally to dance the last dance at the hotel, like a feudal lord. At the end of the novel, the man in white is exposed as a mercenary old anti-Semitic Californian, but Win Berry, symbolically blind, never sees him as he really is. The capacity to dream, despite all the evidence that the world is a harsh and cruel place, Irving implies, is an invaluable quality, one that makes Win Berry and his children, like Jay Gatsby, worth more than all the rest of the people they confront. The point is made in another *Gatsby*-like allusion, a passage in which John Berry encounters, in the middle of a New York street, the villain of the novel, the football hero and successful member of the establishment Chipper Dove, who many years earlier had led a gang rape of John's beloved sister Franny. The chance meeting leads to a denouement through which Franny and John wreak a bizarre vengeance on Chipper Dove and thus is not similar to the final encounter of Nick Carraway and Tom Buchanan; but in the context of the rest of the *Gatsby*-esque matter that pervades *The Hotel New Hampshire,* John's encounter with Chipper is surely not without its tribute to Fitzgerald.

Many other American novels pay homage to the impress of *The Great Gatsby*. Those works that are surveyed here, both major and minor, acclaim the qualities that Fitzgerald's contemporaries and scholars and critics have found of high and lasting merit in *Gatsby*: a mastery of language as it is exhibited in style and technique; a brilliant capacity to make a fictive, imagined world come alive, both in its details and in its people. Perhaps nowhere in the novel does Fitzgerald exhibit these abilities more memorably than in the comic mock-encomium of the guests who attend Gatsby's parties at the beginning of Chapter 4. One of the striking manifestations of force of *The Great Gatsby* in modern American fiction is that other novels have imitated the device of Nick's guest list. To Gatsby's house of fiction have come Thomas Wolfe in *Look Homeward, Angel* (1929) and James Baldwin in *Tell Me How Long the Train's Been Gone* (1968).[55] William Styron came closest to Fitzgerald's combination of irony and social realism in *Lie Down in Darkness* (1951). Here is Styron describing the guests at the wedding parties of his young female protagonist (ellipses are editorial):

> There was Admiral Ernest Lovelace, who was the naval inspector at the shipyard; he had lost his wife in an automobile accident two years ago. There were the Muncys and the Cuthberts and the Heger-

tys. . . . Old Carter Houston himself was there, along with his wife, who remained a Virginia belle at the age of seventy and pronounced Carter "Cyatah". . . . There were the Appletons and the La Farges and the Fauntleroy Mayos, who were F.F.V.'s; and the Martin Braunsteins, who were Jews. . . . Doctors Holcomb and Schmidt and J. E. B. Stuart and Lonergan and Bulwinkle (they all smelled faintly of ether) – and there was Dr. Pruitt Delaplane, making his first hesitant public appearance after his trial and acquittal for criminal abortion. . . .[56]

The long shadow of Jay Gatsby has faded from the lawns of West Egg, but it falls more and more deeply across the hearts and minds of each succeeding generation of American readers and writers. Like Gatsby, even the most hardheaded Americans conceive of themselves (whether correctly is not the point) as idealists whose dreams can be made true, as eternal youths whose innocence can never really be lost, as magicians who can mesmerize the world into accepting their dreams. Fitzgerald, in tapping that cultural myth, made *The Great Gatsby* an American – indeed, a world – classic, a persistent and permanent presence in American culture.

NOTES

1 New York: Farrar & Rinehart, 1944, pp. 148–9.

2 New York: St. Martin's, 1984, p. 194.

3 Boston: Houghton Mifflin, 1951.

4 New York: Random House, 1950.

5 "Pasting It Together," in *The Crack-Up*, ed. Edmund Wilson (New York: New Directions, 1945), p. 81.

6 Sheilah Graham and Gerold Frank, *Beloved Infidel: The Education of a Woman* (New York: Holt, 1958).

7 Sheilah Graham, *The Rest of the Story* (New York: Coward-McCann, 1964), pp. 248–55.

8 *Fitzgerald Newsletter*, ed. Matthew J. Bruccoli (Washington, D.C.: Microcard Editions, 1969), pp. 5–6.

9 Clive Barnes, "Theater: Hunter's 'Scott and Zelda,'" *New York Times*, January 8, 1974, p. 27.

10 New York: Dramatists Play Service, 1981.

11 For a full examination of the incident, see Matthew J. Bruccoli, *Scott*

and Ernest: The Fitzgerald–Hemingway Friendship (New York: Random House, 1978), pp. 130–5.

12 Ernest Hemingway, "Scott Fitzgerald," "Hawks Do Not Share" and "A Matter of Measurement," *A Moveable Feast* (New York: Scribners, 1964).

13 Boston: Little, Brown, 1969.

14 Boston: Little, Brown, 1977.

15 See William F. Nolan's review in *Fitzgerald/Hemingway Annual 1978*, ed. Matthew J. Bruccoli and Richard Layman (Detroit: Bruccoli Clark/Gale Research, 1979), pp. 423–5.

16 "F. Scott Fitzgerald," *Atlantic Brief Lives*, ed. Louis Kronenberger (Boston: Little, Brown, 1971), pp. 275–6.

17 Frederick A. Hetzel, "Fitzgerald and Marquand," *Fitzgerald Newsletter*, p. 172.

18 To Dale Warren, November 13, 1950, *Selected Letters of Raymond Chandler*, ed. Frank MacShane (New York: Columbia University Press, 1981), p. 239.

19 Boston: Houghton Mifflin, 1954, p. 89.

20 New York: Grove Press, 1959; in the Evergreen edition, p. 163.

21 "He went on the road, as Jack Kerouac says," *Life*, June 29, 1962, p. 22.

22 *Esquire*, September 1964, pp. 111, 113, 195–6. Reprinted in *Profile of F. Scott Fitzgerald*, ed. Matthew J. Bruccoli (Columbus, Ohio: Merrill, 1971), pp. 107–22.

23 New York: Random House, 1953.

24 *The Portable F. Scott Fitzgerald*, selected by Dorothy Parker (New York: Viking Press, 1945).

25 *Assembly* (New York: Random House, 1961).

26 *Fitzgerald Newsletter*, pp. 151, 318.

27 "Ready or Not, Here Comes *Gatsby*," *Time*, March 18, 1974, pp. 82–91.

28 Matthew J. Bruccoli, *Supplement to F. Scott Fitzgerald: A Descriptive Bibliography* (Pittsburgh: University of Pittsburgh Press, 1980), pp. 164–5.

29 Garden City, N.Y.: Doubleday, Doran, 1935, "Publisher's Note" and pp. 496–99.

30 New York: Harper, 1955, pp. 954–5.

31 New York: Scribners, 1952.

32 London: Whittlesey House/McGraw-Hill, 1946, pp. 368ff.

33 *Fitzgerald Newsletter*, p. 36.

34 Ibid., pp. 5–6.

35 My summary of publication is deeply indebted to two sources: Matthew J. Bruccoli, *Fitzgerald: A Descriptive Bibiography* (Pittsburgh: University of Pittsburgh Press, 1972); and Elaine P. Maimon, "The Biographical Myth of F. Scott Fitzgerald (1940–1970)," unpublished Ph.D. dissertation, University of Pennsylvania, 1970, Appendix, pp. 295, 297. Maimon's appendix is a study of Scribners sales figures for Fitzgerald's books between 1936 and 1968. Unless otherwise noted, subsequent bibliographical and sales information on *The Great Gatsby* is derived from these sources.

36 Jackson R. Bryer, *The Critical Reputation of F. Scott Fitzgerald* (Hamden, Conn.: Archon, 1967), pp. 202–16. Unless otherwise noted, information on scholarship is derived from this source.

37 In addition to my own reading of much of the material, I have drawn upon Jackson R. Bryer, "F. Scott Fitzgerald," *Sixteen Modern American Authors: A Survey of Research and Criticism* (Durham: Duke University Press, 1974), pp. 277–321.

38 My count was made from *The Critical Reputation of F. Scott Fitzgerald* and from *MLA Annual Bibliographies* for the years 1967–82. A study of the range of Fitzgerald between 1950 and 1976 can be seen in Deborah A. Forczek, "Fitzgerald and Hemingway in the Academy: A Survey of Dissertations," *Fitzgerald/Hemingway Annual 1978*, pp. 351–85.

39 Introduction (Durham: Duke University Press, 1972).

40 Boston: Little, Brown, 1951, pp. 182–3; Bantam edition, p. 141.

41 To Mrs. Elizabeth Murray, *Seventy* (New York: House of El Dieff, 1970), item 78. Reprinted as the epigraph to *Profile of F. Scott Fitzgerald*.

42 Boston: Little, Brown, 1955.

43 *Fitzgerald Newsletter*, p. 36. I have not seen this novel.

44 New York: Random House, 1960.

45 *Self-Portrait: Ceaselessly Into the Past* (Santa Barbara: Capra Press, 1981), p. 123.

46 Matthew J. Bruccoli, *Ross Macdonald* (New York: Harcourt Brace Jovanovich, 1984), pp. 32, 80.

47 New York: Alfred A. Knopf, 1965.

48 Boston: Houghton Mifflin, 1968. See Robert Emmet Long, "The Image of Gatsby in the Fiction of Louis Auchincloss and C. D. B. Bryan," *Fitzgerald/Hemingway Annual*, ed. Matthew J. Bruccoli and C. E. Frazer Clark, Jr. (Washington, D.C.: Microcard Editions, 1973), pp. 325–7.

49 Columbia, S.C.: Bruccoli Clark, 1981.

50 New York: Dutton, 1970, p. 31.

51 New York: Simon & Schuster, 1973, p. 175.
52 New York: Norton, 1977.
53 New York: Dell, 1981, pp. 140, 144.
54 New York: Dutton, 1981.
55 See Robert Emmet Long, "The Vogue of Gatsby's Guest List," *Fitzgerald/Hemingway Annual 1969*, ed. Matthew J. Bruccoli (Washington, D.C.: Microcard Editions, 1969), pp. 23–5; and Edward Stone, "More ABout Gatsby's Guest List," *Fitzgerald/Hemingway Annual 1969*, pp. 315–16.
56 Indianapolis: Bobbs-Merrill, 1951, pp. 260–1.

3

Money, Love, and Aspiration in *The Great Gatsby*

ROGER LEWIS

ONE characteristic of popular American fiction is the implicit separation of love and money. Possession of one does not lead to possession of the other. If the protagonists of Horatio Alger's books become rich and win the girl, such winning is an adjunct to their sudden solvency, not a consequence of it. Alger wants his audience to believe, perhaps, that common sense and moral determination secure the love of a worthy partner; but that these qualities of common sense and moral determination are the property of those who must struggle for money is an assumption – not an issue Alger wants to explore. As a result, it is impossible to imagine what happens to Ragged Dick, Frank Fowler, or any of the hundreds of Horatio Alger heroes after their first success.

The separation of love and money characterizes serious American fiction too. The guilt that seems to lurk behind the source of Lambert Strether's wealth (the firm in Woollett "made something") underscores both his and, I suspect, his creator's distaste for tainting the finer emotions with anything so crass as commercialism. If the independence and energy that constitute Strether's as well as his earlier prototype's, Christopher Newman's, most appealing facets come from contact with the struggles of business, the novel prefers to treat this matter as background. The inamoratas of Strether and Newman are fascinating more for their richness of background and their exquisiteness of taste than for the fortune that sustains these qualities.

What I have said so far seems to me to hold especially true for American fiction before World War I. The laissez-faire democratic ideal that America has always believed it believed is the product of an age when individual effort counted, when a man could rise by his own efforts, and when – if his affairs were not succeeding – he

41

could at least escape by signing up for a whaling voyage or lighting out for the territory ahead of the rest. When the system failed, it was the fault of rapscallions and crooks; the vision itself remained an ideal and the standard from which criticisms and judgments could be made.

World War I shattered this vision. It ended once and for all the faith in individual effort that had been eroding since the Industrial Revolution and had persisted – sometimes naively and sometimes defensively – in the fiction that I have been mentioning. As Mark Schorer has pointed out, disillusionment with the American system and the efficacy of individual effort is the distinguishing characteristic of postwar American writing.[1]

Of course, not many, if any, ideals die totally and suddenly even after mortal blows, and during periods of transition the most complex and seminal works are often written. In this respect the 1920s bridge the gap between the older, simpler, more naive and idealistic America and the bewildering, disparate, rootless, cynical America of the present. *The Great Gatsby*, neatly published in the mid-1920s, is a key work, looking Janus-like in both directions.

The opening words of the novel express this double vision.

> In my younger and more vulnerable years my father gave me some advice that I've been turning over in my mind ever since.
> "Whenever you feel like criticising any one," he told me, "just remember that all the people in this world haven't had the advantages that you've had." (p. 1)

The narrator, Nick Carraway, senses that he is too quick to condemn; his father has a perspective from which to make judgments. Nick has to remind himself of his father's more balanced, human appraisal. The younger Carraway has one foot in the past and one in the present; his allegiance to his father's older, more careful manner is maintained at the cost of constant surveillance.

When, in a following paragraph, Nick declares that after returning from the East he "wanted the world to be in uniform and at a sort of moral attention forever" (p. 2), he connects the war with his cynical, guilty disapproval of the New York the book is about to portray, but he goes on to make an exception for Gatsby, allying Gatsby to an older, more humane America – an ironic identifica-

tion, since Gatsby "represented everything for which I have un-
affected scorn" (p. 2). Thus, not only the narrator but also Gatsby
is double, making the novel doubly double.

Such doubleness is important, because by it Fitzgerald creates a
character whose naiveté can be simultaneously touching and absurd, and who can possess the most romantic and crass attitudes at
the same time. By the end of the novel, Gatsby and what he stands
for reach proportions of mythic profundity.

Expressing such resonances was a talent Fitzgerald had to develop. Some indication of his abilities is present in *This Side of Paradise*, and some of the rhythms of *The Great Gatsby* appear in embry-
onic form in the earlier book, but it is not until "Winter Dreams"
in 1923 that Fitzgerald explicitly connects the themes of love and
money. In this story, Dexter Green, a figure straight from the work
ethic of Horatio Alger, loses Judy Jones, a child of wealth.

Yet the relationship between love and money in "Winter
Dreams" is not as simple as in Alger. For one thing, Judy Jones, the
heroine of the story, is a romantically attractive woman. In Horatio
Alger's fiction, rich females are cold and cruel and loveless, but
Judy Jones is exciting and desirable, capable of exciting love in
others, but, once society has corrupted her, not herself capable of
loving. Exciting others and promising love, however, matter more
than the realizable dreams of wealth necessary to obtain Judy
Jones; they give the story all its powerful emotion. The intan-
gibility of the emotion, its transience and fragility, its evanescent
illusory quality, and the fact that it is unrealizable account for its
enchantment. What sustains the charm is the atmosphere that
surrounds Judy Jones, an atmosphere engendered by wealth. This
wealth destroys even as it creates; thus, the doubleness of Gatsby is
prefigured here.

When Dexter Green is aware of how empty and bereft his life is
because the dream of the old Judy Jones has gone, he has the
impulse to "get very drunk." There are shades here of Amory
Blaine, who similarly responds when Rosalind is not to be his. But
not, seemingly, shades of Gatsby; although a bootlegger, Gatsby is
abstemious and careful – a man aware of his own doubleness.
Both dreamer and vulgarian at the same time, he is, like Dexter

Green, a money maker and a romantic; unlike Dexter Green, he seems to balance between the two. He appears able to keep the halves in control.

Almost predictably, the object of Gatsby's romantic quest, Daisy Buchanan, comes to us in a double way. She is, of course, presented not by Gatsby or Fitzgerald but by Nick Carraway, and she comes to us through his filter of contradictory impressions and emotions. After Nick's description of Tom, with the latter's conceit and meanness, the reader is prepared to respond instantly to the charm of Daisy. Daisy comes to us laughing "an absurd, charming little laugh" (p. 10) that makes Nick laugh also. The pleasing impression of Daisy is largely vocal:

> . . . there was an excitement in her voice that men who had cared for her found difficult to forget: a singing compulsion, a whispered "Listen," a promise that she had done gay, exciting things just a while since and that there were gay, exciting things hovering in the next hour. (p. 11)

But then Nick's doubleness reasserts itself. Just as we are seduced by her simpering mockery of her husband, captivated by her posturing, her "thrilling scorn" (p. 21), and the romantic glow with which Fitzgerald has surrounded her, Nick pulls us back.

> The instant her voice broke off, ceasing to compel my attention, my belief, I felt the basic insincerity of what she had said. It made me uneasy, as though the whole evening had been a trick of some sort to exact a contributory emotion from me. I waited, and sure enough, in a moment she looked at me with an absolute smirk on her lovely face, as if she had asserted her membership in a rather distinguished secret society to which she and Tom belonged. (pp. 21–2)

This identification with Tom comes as a surprise. So does its limited extension to Nick himself. (A few pages earlier, Nick has referred to the fact that he and Tom "were in the same senior society" [p. 9] at Yale.) The three-way identification of Tom, Nick, and Daisy momentarily demystifies Daisy and consequently makes the reader trust more in Nick's judgments. Nick can both glamorize Daisy so that the reader shares Gatsby's attraction to her and undercut Daisy so that the reader can see her from without. Such a set of contradictions strengthens the spell Daisy can cast and gives us a view of Daisy that contrasts to the one Gatsby will later present.

The double view of Daisy persists throughout the novel, although it is later replaced by the more compelling topic of Gatsby's feeling for her; it certainly continues through Chapter 5, when Gatsby meets Daisy again after five years. At this point, our contradictory feelings are transferred to their relationship. Fitzgerald deliberately recalls our reactions by a reference to the first scene with Daisy when Nick refers to a joke about the butler's nose. His description of Daisy's voice when Gatsby enters Nick's house, also recalls that previous episode:

> For half a minute there wasn't a sound. Then from the living-room I heard a sort of choking murmur and part of a laugh, followed by Daisy's voice on a clear artificial note:
> "I certainly am awfully glad to see you again." (p. 104)

Just when it seems as though the hollow, mannered, deliberate falseness is going to continue, Fitzgerald effects another peripeteia. When Nick returns after having left Daisy and Gatsby alone for awhile, Daisy is crying, and "every vestige of embarrassment" (p. 107) has disappeared. Daisy's throat, at this point, "full of aching, grieving beauty, told only of her unexpected joy" (p. 108). Love seems possible, especially for Gatsby. He dominates the rest of the chapter, as "a new well-being radiated from him" (p. 108).

It is no accident that this scene falls squarely in the middle of the novel. It might also be the emotional center of it, and it is noteworthy that in a letter to his editor, Maxwell Perkins, Fitzgerald mentioned this scene as his favorite.[2]

Yet, moving as it may be, the initial encounter of Gatsby and Daisy cannot really be the emotional center of *The Great Gatsby*. For one thing, however much we may be charmed by Daisy, Nick's previous depiction of her undercuts our ability to give unquestioning credence to her feelings on this occasion. And, more comically, the means by which Gatsby expresses his feelings for Daisy – even though those feelings are sincere – is by showing off his possessions. Urging Daisy and Nick to explore his house, he tells them: " 'It took me just three years to earn the money that bought it' " (p. 109). The very language in which Nick describes Gatsby's love for Daisy is commercial: "I think he revalued everything in his house

45

according to the measure of response it drew from her well-loved eyes" (p. 111). Daisy responds to Gatsby's display: she cries over his beautiful shirts.

Even when the sentiments are genuine, they are formulated in monetary terms. Gatsby's love for Daisy is an intense and worked-out variety of that which lovers of all ages have felt; its expression is distinctively that of postwar America, of a society that consumes.

At this point in *The Great Gatsby* the relationship between love and money has been suggested but not enlarged, as it will be later. For one thing, we do not know about Gatsby's impoverished beginnings, and our ignorance is essential to Fitzgerald's plan. It is not simply the case, as Edith Wharton suggested in a letter to Fitzgerald, that Fitzgerald wishes to tell his story in a new fashion just to be "modern"[3]; nor can I wholly accept Fitzgerald's explanation that the reason for withholding Gatsby's past is to augment the sense of mystery surrounding him,[4] although doing so does have such an effect. Rather, withholding exactly who Gatsby is or where he comes from is a method of underscoring the rootlessness of postwar American society, its restless alienation, and its consequent reliance on money as a code for expressing emotions and identity.

Fitzgerald seems at every point to emphasize the unconnectedness of Gatsby. Gatsby has shifting identities according to which party guest one listens to, but most of the identities, even the one that turns out to be "true," have something of the unreal or fantastic about them. When they do not, they seem fantastic by being juxtaposed with others that do.

> "Who is he?" I demanded. "Do you know?"
> "He's just a man named Gatsby."
> "Where is he from, I mean? And what does he do?"
> "Now *you*'re started on the subject," she answered with a wan smile. "Well, he told me once he was an Oxford man."
> A dim background started to take shape behind him, but at her next remark it faded away.
> "However, I don't believe it." (p. 59)

This rootlessness begins when the war ends. Before he identifies himself, the war is the subject of Gatsby's conversation with Nick, and it is the most grounded identity, until the novel's denouement, that Gatsby has.

How do the members of such a rootless, mobile, indifferent society acquire a sense of who they are? Most of them don't. The novel presents large numbers of them as comic, disembodied names of guests at dinner parties: the Chromes, the Backhyssons, and the Dennickers. Some, of course, have some measure of fame, but even Jordan Baker's reputation does not do much for her other than get her entrée to more parties. A very few, such as Gatsby, stand out by their wealth; his hospitality secures him a hold on many peoples' memories, but Fitzgerald is quick to point up the emptiness of this: Klipspringer cares more about his lost tennis shoes than Gatsby's death.

In this connection, Fitzgerald's insistence on Gatsby as a man who "sprang from his own Platonic conception of himself" is important. Conceiving one's self would seem to be a final expression of rootlessness. And it has other consequences for love, money, and aspirations as well. When one's sense of self is self-created, when one is present at one's own creation, so to speak, one is in a paradoxical position. One knows everything about oneself that can be known, and yet the significance of such knowledge is unclear, for no outside contexts exist to create meaning. The result is that a self-created man turns to the past, for he can know that. It is an inescapable context. For Gatsby and for the novel, the past is crucial.

His sense of the past as something that he not only knows but also thinks he can control sets Gatsby apart from Nick and gives him mythical, larger-than-life dimensions. When he tells Nick that "'of course'" the past can be repeated (p. 133) or that Tom's love for Daisy was "'just personal'" (p. 182), he may be compensating for his inability to recapture Daisy; but he must believe these things because the postwar world in which he, Gatsby, lives is meaningless and almost wholly loveless.

A glance at the relationships in *The Great Gatsby* proves this latter point. Daisy and Tom's marriage has gone dead; they must cover their dissatisfactions with the distractions of the idle rich. Myrtle and Tom are using one another; Myrtle hates George, who is too dull to understand her; the McKees exist in frivolous and empty triviality. Even Nick seems unsure about his feelings for the tennis girl back in the Midwest. His attraction to Jordan Baker is clearly an extension of this earlier relationship (both girls are associated with sports), but occurring as it does in the East, it partakes of the East's corruption. It too calls forth the need for money. In a draft manuscript of *The Great Gatsby*, Nick makes the link between money and desire explicit: "I thought that I loved her and I wanted money with a sudden physical pang."[5] Later Nick compares his loveless affair with Jordan to refuse the sea might sweep away, a feeling that Jordan senses and throws back at Nick with cruel irony when she accuses him of being dishonest – leading her on with no intention of marrying her – after lying to him that she is engaged to another man.

In brief, the world of *The Great Gatsby* can seem as sordid, loveless, commercial, and dead as the ash heaps presided over by the eyes of Dr. T. J. Eckleburg. Indeed, this atmosphere is so essential to *The Great Gatsby* that one of the alternative titles Fitzgerald considered for the novel was *Among the Ash-Heaps and Millionaires*.

Against this backdrop, the Gatsby–Daisy relationship seems to shine. It is at least a shared connection in which both partners respond with equal intensity. For Gatsby it has endured: He has loved Daisy for five years. And if their love is founded upon feelings from the past, these give it, notwithstanding Gatsby's insistence on being able to repeat the past, an inviolability. It exists in the world of money and corruption but is not of it.

Some implications of the inviolability Gatsby does not see. His very protesting, however, shows his sense of the impossibility of returning and makes at once more poignant and more desperate his effort to win Daisy – a poignancy further increased by the futility of his money in achieving this end.

> "I'm going to fix everything just the way it was before," he said, nodding determinedly. "She'll see."
> He talked a lot about the past, and I gathered that he wanted to recover something, some idea of himself perhaps, that had gone into loving Daisy. His life had been confused and disordered since then, but if he could once return to a certain starting place and go over it all slowly, he could find out what that thing was. . . . (p. 133).

The last orderly period of Gatsby's life, then, was the period before he was sent to fight in the war, when he was still in the process of self-creation. The period when he loved Daisy and when Daisy loved him preceded his period of fabulous wealth. In this respect, he fits the Alger stereotype.

The period when his love becomes most intense, however, is precisely that in which he does not see Daisy. The love born in this period is therefore largely a function of his imagination. The kernel of his experience remains untouched because it is safely embedded in a previous time; the growth of the love is wild and luxuriant. It spurs him on, resulting in the glamorous world of parties and in the "huge incoherent failure" (p. 217) of his house.

The romantic and fantastic nature of Gatsby's love seems extraordinary and absurd, looked at in worldy, practical terms. Why does he wait so long to arrange a meeting and then use Jordan Baker and Nick Carraway to bring it about? A man with Gatsby's resources would surely have a hundred easier ways to do what he does in the course of this story. The answer is that the love becomes *more* important than the object of it. Gatsby has already started down this path in Louisville when he asks himself, "'What would be the use of doing great things if I could have a better time telling her what I was going to do?'" (p. 180).

If Gatsby himself is presented as curiously "unreal," the connection between Daisy and Gatsby — the unobtainable and the insubstantial — is destined to founder in a world as insistently material as the one Fitzgerald details for us. In such a world, Gatsby cannot make love to Daisy. Even earlier, during the war, when Gatsby and Daisy did make love ("took" her [p. 178]), physical contact was a limitation of his love: "He knew that when he kissed this girl, and forever wed his unutterable visions to her perishable breath, his mind would never romp again like the mind of God" (p. 134). And the moments of greatest intimacy between them are those when they neither speak nor make love: "They had never been closer in their month of love, nor communicated more profoundly one with another, than when she brushed silent lips against his coat's shoulder or when he touched the end of her fingers, gently, as though she were asleep" (p. 180). No wonder, then, that after the five-year hiatus, when Gatsby's love has had the chance to

feed upon itself and nourish itself, the possibility of physical intimacy has not grown, but the love has grown beyond the merely
"personal."

For these reasons Chapter 7, where Daisy, Tom, Gatsby, Nick
and Jordan engage a suite at the Plaza hotel, is of greatest importance. If Daisy's love for Gatsby is to endure, it must exist in non–
Platonic, physical terms. It must exist in the world of money. The
scene in New York demonstrates the impossibility of this transfor-
mation and further connects Gatsby's love to his sense of fabulous,
mythical riches.

If Gatsby dominates the first meeting with Daisy – the chapter
ends at his house, on his territory – Tom dominates the denouement at the hotel. The change of venue allies Chapter 7 to Chapter
2, the scene of Tom's violent party with Myrtle Wilson, a connection Fitzgerald underscores by the telephone conversation about
Tom Buchanan's selling his car and by the stopping for gasoline at
George Wilson's station.

Daisy sees purposelessness as characterizing her whole life:
"'What'll we do with ourselves this afternoon?' cried Daisy, 'and
the day after that, and the next thirty years?'" (p. 141). The idle-
ness of this remark doesn't threaten Gatsby's grandiose feelings,
but Daisy inhabits the physical world of Tom, and she wants to act,
not just dream, so it is she who proposes that the party move to
New York – to Tom's territory. Such a move takes the day away
from Gatsby. Daisy's voice ominously molds the "senselessness [of
the heat] into forms" (p. 142) – i.e., abstract feelings into concrete
deeds.

It is before the five characters move to New York that Gatsby
makes his famous remark to Nick: "'Her voice is full of money'"
(p. 144). This insight, which Fitzgerald added when the novel was
in galley proof, shows Gatsby's understanding of the link between
love and money. Daisy's voice has been described as the seductive,
thrilling aspect of her. What Gatsby, with surprising consciousness, states is that Daisy's charm is allied to the attraction of
wealth; money and love hold similar attractions.

It is true that from Wolfsheim to Nick Carraway, people are in
the East to earn their livings, to pursue "the shining secrets that

only Midas and Morgan and Maecenas knew" (p. 5). But Gatsby, with his boundless capacity for love, a capacity unique in the sterile world he inhabits, sees that the pursuit of money is a substitute for love. He knows himself well enough to see that his own attraction toward wealth is tied to his love for Daisy. The fact that Gatsby's money, like his love, should be self-made gives his description of her voice authority and depth.

That Daisy's voice should be full of money is a remark only Gatsby could make. It is a statement of someone alive to the possibilities of love and money and sensitive to them – perhaps too much so. Tom could never have provided the description of Daisy. His attraction to Daisy has nothing to do with her wealth. (Her family is well off, but apparently not very rich – certainly not compared to the Buchanan fortune.) And it is impossible to imagine Tom making Gatsby's remark because Tom is accustomed to having money. Money *qua* money holds no interest for him because it does not have to be chased after: His is old money simply there to be used. Tom may buy anything he wishes – from polo ponies to cufflinks – but he understands that polo ponies or cufflinks are all he is buying. His money was divested of dreams before he was even born.

Gatsby's, on the other hand, is new money, money in the process of being acquired. This newness gives the money some purpose and vitality; what Gatsby buys he buys for a purpose: to win Daisy. But there is a danger for Gatsby in this redeeming purposefulness. When he buys his fantastic house, he thinks he is buying a dream, not simply purchasing property. This direction makes Gatsby a more sympathetic man than Tom, but it is a sympathy he projects at the price of naiveté; he is completely innocent of the limits of what money can do, a man who, we feel, would believe every word of an advertisement. Daisy even makes this identification: "'You resemble the advertisement of the man'" (p. 142).

In this respect Gatsby embodies the acquisitive, consuming spirit of the rest of the characters in the novel. The characters of *The Great Gatsby* are pursuing a world of misunderstood elegance, mirrored in a thousand romantic and comic details and apotheosized, perhaps, in Nick's description of New York as made of "white heaps and sugar lumps all built with a wish out of non-olfactory money" (p. 82).

"Non-olfactory" is a curious word. It is Fitzgerald's way of using the common locution that "money smells." He is also reminding us, of course, that Gatsby's money does not "smell" right – however explicitly or tacitly condoned by the denizens of Gatsby's world, illegal and shifty means (bootlegging, stolen securities) have been used to make that wealth. Gatsby does not see that the corruption at the base of his fortune in effect compromises his vision of life with Daisy. You cannot win the ideal with the corrupt, and you cannot buy integrity or taste with dollars. When late in the story Daisy attends one of Gatsby's parties, she is repelled rather than attracted.

So stated, this has a moralistic ring, but no reader of *The Great Gatsby* could ever mistake it for a didactic work. The reader is at many points encouraged to marvel at the glitter, especially as it is the means by which Gatsby chases after Daisy. If such morality as the book conveys comes through most explicitly in the attitudes of its narrator, there are nevertheless many moments when Nick is simply overwhelmed by the astonishing freshness and strength of Gatsby's feeling. Indeed, after the remark about Daisy's voice, Nick finds himself participating in Gatsby's thinking. He finds this moment similar to an earlier one in Chapter 5 when he "was going to ask to see the rubies" (p. 113). He continues Gatsby's dream for us, recognizing the strength of Gatsby's identification of Daisy's voice and money.

> That was it. I'd never understood it before. It was full of money – that was the inexhaustible charm that rose and fell in it, the jingle of it, the cymbals' song of it. . . . High in a white palace the king's daughter, the golden girl. . . . (p. 144)

Here not only Nick but also we share Gatsby's dream. The man who has asked Daisy, "'Can't you talk about crops or something?'" (p. 15) breaks into reverie. We share in the pleasures, in the fantasies; Nick's and Gatsby's vision becomes ours. And thus the book fosters our appreciation of Gatsby's corrupt dream. Yet such participation can never be wholehearted and can never be complete: Nick breaks off as Tom returns with a bottle of whiskey, and the scene becomes Tom's again.

The novel's insistence that Tom win the struggle over Daisy is tantamount to denying the realization of the kind of love that Gatsby is offering Daisy and that the novel values above all others. What does remain is the marriage of Tom and Daisy. Ironically, such love as even that relationship may contain is embedded in the past ("that day I carried you down from the Punch Bowl'" [p. 159]). The future, uncertain and without love, is a kind of death – rendering the world of *The Great Gatsby* grim indeed. Nick sees the oncoming years as harrowing and lonely ones. What does life hold for a decent man like Nick? He has no love, unlike Gatsby. Nick is thirty, a number that recalls Daisy's frightening question, "'What'll we do with ourselves . . . for the next thirty years?'" (p. 144)

One answer to Nick's self-doubts might be his liaison with Jordan Baker. That, however, has already been presented to us as a troubled one. If Jordan is "too wise ever to carry well-forgotten dreams from age to age" (p. 163), she is wrapped in almost impenetrable narcissism; after the disturbing events of the day when Myrtle has been killed, Jordan is ready for a date: "'It's only half-past nine'" (p. 171). But Nick, having watched Gatsby's love for Daisy effectively terminated, having seen Myrtle violently run down, and wrapped in his own loneliness, cannot accede to compulsive and indeed perverse socializing.

The novel's sense of duality, of attraction and repellence, diminishes after the hotel scene. Instead the book proceeds with deliberate mechanicalness to work out the consequences of Daisy's having run down Myrtle. Wilson's dull, self-defensive grief is the embodiment of the sterility of the valley of ashes; lacking a dream, his life itself is a kind of death. Wilson may have been married in a church "'a long time ago,'" (p. 189), but his present God is the disembodied eyes of Dr. T. J. Eckleburg, an advertisement. For him love has vanished, and he is left without a vision to sustain him. The man who kills Gatsby is already dead when he commits the murder; Nick Carraway describes him as "ashen" (p. 194), and his suicide is simply a belated acknowledgment of his condition.

Wilson and Gatsby both die by Wilson's hand, suggesting an identification. There is one. Both have aspired to marry above their social station. Whereas Wilson borrows a suit for his wedding to conceal his low economic status, Gatsby wears his country's uniform while courting Daisy. But there the similarity ends. Yet it is worth noting that Gatsby has tried to do what probably no other developed male character in a major work of American fiction has tried to do. He has tried to marry for love into a class higher than the one he comes from. Usually women make such an attempt, namely, Sister Carrie, Lily Bart, and a host of others.

In this respect the difference between Gatsby and the hero of another book published in the same year, Theodore Dreiser's *An American Tragedy,* is instructive. Clyde Griffiths, like Gatsby, tries to rise from humble beginnings in the Midwest to a larger, more glamorous life in the East. Like Gatsby, Clyde attaches himself to a woman (Sondra Finchley) from a moneyed family. And both believe that if they only have enough money, they can buy the dream they seek.

There is a crucial difference. Clyde Griffiths is sexually attracted to Sondra Finchley, but he is not in love with her. Sondra provides the wealth and glamor that Clyde's lover Roberta, is unable to, but Clyde's feelings for Sondra are really subordinate to his sense of pleasure in her leisured environment. Of Gatsby's depth of feeling, of Gatsby's imagination, of Gatsby's genuineness of sentiment ("'I can't describe to you how surprised I was to find out I loved her, old sport'" [p. 179]), Clyde Griffiths knows nothing.

He is unaware of the fact, but Clyde is using Sondra for his own ends. Jay Gatsby is not using Daisy. He strives to move in higher circles because Daisy is there. Of course, in doing so, he violates a cultural norm. He tries to buy into a tradition instead of accepting one. Social convention and time triumph. The wearing away of freedom and the impossibility of realizing the only dreams that make life worth living are the themes of *The Great Gatsby*. The absence of great love is more painful because the sense of possibility money provides is so powerfully ambient in Gatsby's world.

Again, because the dream is unrealizable, the past becomes increasingly important to the book, for it is in memories that the dream can live. The final pages of the novel are pervaded by the consciousness of the past and the sense of history ("the dark fields of the republic" [p. 218]). For most readers these pages are the most moving and suggestive in the book, and, many would add, in the whole of F. Scott Fitzgerald's writing. The reason is that what has been felt or implied in every line earlier in the novel is expanded there in paragraphs of increasingly greater suggestiveness until the passage achieves archetypical resonances – resonances beyond even the usual national, historical ones claimed for this section of the novel.

That these final paragraphs should echo through the whole book can be illustrated bibliographically. Nick's meditation about American history and the sense of possibility originally appeared in the manuscript not as the conclusion to the whole novel, but as the end of Chapter 1, where Nick returns to West Egg from visiting Tom and Daisy and sees Gatsby attempting to "determine what share was his of our local heavens" (p. 26). All the images from the final pages – the moon rising higher, the "inessential houses" (p. 217), the "fresh, green breast of the new world" (p. 217), and so on are here, and the passage's haunting, lost feeling comes through because of them. Nick's accidental sighting of Gatsby at this point is not sufficient reason for the depth or length of the meditation, and Fitzgerald brilliantly repositioned the passage to where it now stands – but the feeling of loss was already present early in the conception. If in reading the book we find the final paragraphs a fitting conclusion, then that is so as a result of the novel's originally having hung from them, or having been composed with them already written.

From the start, therefore, Fitzgerald sensed the possibility of writing a novel whose theme embraced the notion of dreams in a general way. In letters written around the period of *The Great Gatsby*, Fitzgerald refers to the novel's being about those illusions that matter so much that you chase after them, because even though they are illusions, nothing matters as much as they do. What counts is nothing less than the profoundest experience of love. Yet what is Gatsby's love for Daisy but illusion, one fed by the dream of fulfillment America offered?

> And as the moon rose higher the inessential houses began to melt away until gradually I became aware of the old island here that flowered once for Dutch sailors' eyes – a fresh, green breast of the new world. Its vanished trees, the trees that had made way for

> Gatsby's house, had once pandered in whispers to the last and
> greatest of all human dreams; for a transitory enchanted moment
> man must have held his breath in the presence of this continent,
> compelled into an aesthetic contemplation he neither understood
> nor desired, face to face for the last time in history with something
> commensurate to his capacity for wonder. (pp. 217–18)

The love that imbues this passage, the warmth and closeness of the
tone, is expressed in the imagery of birth, from the womblike
feeling of holding breath, from the breast of the new world, and
from the lack of understanding or desire: All these are feelings
connected with being born. And because every man, including the
reader, is the "last" man in history while he is alive, these sentences achieve the immediacy of myth and archetype.

The love that Gatsby has for Daisy is one whose sexual compo-
nent is hidden in the inviolate past. It sees the affairs of the world
as necessary but sordid. It is the love Fitzgerald felt for America, as
Alfred Kazin has noted in *An American Procession*.[6] In such en-
closed dreams we are children; they offer us a kind of ultimate
innocence. But because such love is unconsummated and uncon-
summatable, it cannot express itself directly. Instead it imbues that
which surrounds it with its own special quality.

This quality spills into Nick's sense of history and into the
novel's feelings of what it means to be wealthy. Unsophisticated
writers such as Horatio Alger made a false separation between love
and money; more complex writers sublimated or subordinated the
one to the other. The unique contribution of *The Great Gatsby* is the
identification of them. The acquisition of money and love are both
part of the same dream, the will to return to the quintessential
unity that exists only at birth and at death.

The last sentence of the novel, "So we beat on, boats against the
current, borne back ceaselessly into the past," points out that all of
our great dreams are grounded in impossibility: We progress toward that which we want, but the natural movement of life is
retrograde – we die. The water here, as in *The Waste Land*, is both
life-giving amnion and a destroying force.

To say this as Fitzgerald has is to reach an insight of final proportion. For this reason, *The Great Gatsby* transcends the ideas of the
1920s, its ostensible subject. By yoking the harsher, cynical post-

war judgments about love and human endeavor to the older dreams of the past, the novel makes a synthesis greater than any single period could have achieved. *The Great Gatsby* is about love and money, but its greater subject — the tragic nature of aspiration — links these two in ways that deepen in the broadest, profoundest way our sense of who we are.

NOTES

1 Mark Schorer, *Sinclair Lewis: An American Life* (New York: McGraw-Hill, 1961), p. 246.
2 Circa December 1, 1924. *The Letters of F. Scott Fitzgerald*, ed. Andrew Turnbull (New York: Scribners, 1963), p. 170.
3 "Three Letters about *The Great Gatsby*," *The Crack-Up*, ed. Edmund Wilson (New York: New Directions, 1945), p. 309.
4 To Maxwell Perkins, January 24, 1925. *Letters*, pp. 175–6.
5 F. Scott Fitzgerald, *A Facsimile of the Manuscript*, ed. Matthew J. Bruccoli (Washington, D.C.: Bruccoli Clark/Microcard, 1973), p. 123.
6 Alfred Kazin, *An American Procession* (New York: Knopf, 1984), p. 393.

4

The Idea of Order at West Egg

SUSAN RESNECK PARR

PPROXIMATELY ten years after *The Great Gatsby* was published, F. Scott Fitzgerald observed in *The Crack-Up* that "the test of a first-rate intelligence is the ability to hold two opposed ideas in the mind at the same time, and still retain the ability to function." He then elaborated, "One should, for example, be able to see that things are hopeless and yet be determined to make them otherwise."[1]

Fitzgerald went on to apply this "general observation" to his own life a decade earlier, that is, to the time when he would have been writing *Gatsby*:

> Life, ten years ago, was largely a personal matter. I must hold in balance the sense of the futility of effort and the sense of the necessity to struggle; the conviction of the inevitability of failure and still the determination to "succeed" – and, more than these, the contradiction between the dead hand of the past and the high intentions of the future.[2]

Fitzgerald was also explicit that at earlier points in his life, after personal failures and disappointments, he had come to feel that "there was a vast irresponsibility toward every obligation, a deflation of all my values. A passionate belief in order, a disregard of motives or consequences in favor of guesswork and prophecy, a feeling that craft and industry would have a place in any world. . . ."[3]

These remarks are important because of what they reveal about Fitzgerald's own state of mind at various times in his life. They are also important, I believe, because they help illuminate Fitzgerald's approach to the question of how the conscious individual comes to terms with the sense of hopelessness and human vulnerability that, in the case of *The Great Gatsby*, seems to be the product of an awareness of time's movement, on the one hand, and the belief that the modern world provides neither order nor meaning, on the other hand. Even more specifically, as I will argue in the pages to follow, in *Gatsby* — as in the essays of *The Crack-Up* — Fitzgerald suggests that the conscious individual can function best if he or she can reconcile and accept "opposed ideas." Within the novel, these "opposed ideas" are embodied in a series of paradoxes.[4]

The first of these paradoxes is that the major characters in the novel again and again embrace illusions that they know to be illusions in order to cope with their sense of hopelessness and vulnerability. The second paradox is that the illusions they embrace are rooted typically in their pasts, even though, as Nick Carraway knows and as many of the others so painfully come to understand, " 'You can't repeat the past' " (p. 133). The final paradox is an outgrowth of the first two — that even as the novel makes it understandable why individuals would embrace such illusions, it also makes clear that such a choice is precarious at best because, in the face of time's movement, human frailty, and a modern world that has become a moral and spiritual wasteland, such illusions will not suffice and in fact are likely to be destructive.

In a related matter, the novel's major characters — Gatsby, Daisy, and Nick — quite deliberately assume roles and adopt gestures that they believe are consonant with the illusions they are embracing. All three, in fact, seem to define personality as "an unbroken series of successful gestures" (p. 2). They do so, I would argue, because all three have a passionate belief in order, despite their awareness that time inevitably brings unpredictable and personally threatening changes.

Ironically, this definition of personality as gesture itself contributes to making the world a dangerous place because it reduces human action to mere performance and people to simple players in a game. The implications of such a stance are, as Fitzgerald noted in *The Crack-Up*, to deflate values and to disregard motives and consequences. But just as *The Great Gatsby* dramatizes the devastation that can be wrought when illusions are cherished too long or are made the basis for action, so too does it point to the danger of valuing roles and gestures, however well crafted they may be, at the expense of thought and feeling, of moral choice and moral action.

Early in the novel, Nick Carraway describes himself as being "within and without, simultaneously enchanted and repelled by the inexhaustible variety of life" (p. 43). In that statement and others, Nick suggests his own deeply felt uncertainty about the nature of life's possibilities. In some moments, he is hopeful about what the future might hold and is drawn to the excitement that accompanies change. In other moments, his awareness of human vulnerability overshadows his confidence in life's promise, and so he retreats from whatever situation provokes his anxiety and unhappiness in an effort to exert control and establish a sense of order. That the world around him so often seems chaotic and the people he knows without purpose almost certainly contributes to his ambivalence.

Nick is not the only character in the novel who is conscious of the need to choose whether to be "within or without," whether to embrace life or to try to control it. Gatsby and Daisy, at crucial moments in their lives, evidence a similar awareness and experience a similar ambivalence. All three also respond in the same way, by turning – deliberately and with full awareness – to illusions that they know to be illusions. Gatsby does so when he shapes for himself a new identity and then later when he makes Daisy the embodiment of his dream. Daisy makes similar choices when she marries Tom, not Gatsby, and then again when she abandons Gatsby in order to stay with her husband. And Nick embraces his own illusions when he decides, at the end of the novel, to return home to the Midwest of his childhood.

Nick, in fact, is explicit about how vulnerable people are when faced with a harsh reality that is unadorned by illusion. For example, when he imagines what Gatsby must have felt during the final hours of his life as he waited futilely for a phone call from Daisy, Nick thinks:

> I have an idea that Gatsby himself didn't believe [the phone call] would come, and perhaps he no longer cared. If that was true, he must have felt that he had lost the old warm world, paid a high price for living too long with a single dream. He must have looked

up at an unfamiliar sky through frightening leaves and shivered as
he found what a grotesque thing a rose is and how raw the sunlight
was upon the scarcely created grass. (p. 194)

It is important to emphasize here that Fitzgerald's major characters do not turn to illusions that are separate from the realities of their lives. Rather, the illusions or dreams that seem most vibrant to them are those that transform their everyday realities into something that seems either thrilling or meaningful. Thus, Gatsby's dream turns the green light at the end of Daisy's dock into the most important of his "enchanted objects" (p. 113). His dream also invests his life with meaning as Nick recognizes when he learns of Gatsby's love for Daisy. As Nick describes the moment, "He came alive to me, delivered suddenly from the womb of his purposeless splendor" (p. 95).

As they embrace the various illusions that give shape to their lives, Gatsby, Daisy, and Nick increasingly and deliberately assume roles and adopt gestures that are outgrowths of their illusions. Daisy even goes so far as to value only gestures that are separate from emotion. At Gatsby's party, she is appalled at the "raw vigor" of West Egg and sees as lovely only the pose of the movie star and her director. In Nick's words, "the rest offended her – and inarguably, because it wasn't a gesture but an emotion" (p. 129).

For Gatsby, Daisy, and Nick, this turning to illusion and playing of roles is part of an attempt to recover the vibrancy and promise of their youth. Gatsby, for example, invents for himself an entirely new identity of just the sort "that a seventeen-year-old boy would be likely to invent, and to this conception he was faithful to the end" (p. 118), while Daisy's vision of what her life should be has its origins in her "white girlhood" (p. 24). It is in fact this vision that leads her to marry Tom Buchanan, who can give her a $350,000 string of pearls, instead of waiting for Gatsby, who could offer her only love and hope.

Given the harshness of some of the realities of their adult lives (the war, for Nick and Gatsby; Gatsby's loss of Daisy; and Daisy's awareness of Tom's extramarital affairs), such choices have a certain logic, for only in the innocence of youth were Gatsby, Daisy, and Nick able to have a sense of hope and of life's promise. On the other hand, Nick suggests that even Gatsby, with his "romantic readiness" and his "extraordinary gift for hope" (p. 2), knew from the beginning that whatever beliefs he created for himself were illusory. With a punning and ironic reference to Daisy Fay Buchanan's maiden name, Nick suggests that Gatsby knew that the "promise" of his youthful reveries was "that the rock of the world was founded securely on a fairy's wing" (p. 119).

Gatsby's turning to illusion is the most total of any character in the novel. He also, even more than Nick and Daisy, seems to believe that he can create a personality based on the values of American popular culture. Thus, at the age of seventeen, he defines for himself a completely new identity. As Nick puts it, "The truth was that Jay Gatsby of West Egg, Long Island, sprang from his platonic conception of himself" (p. 118). To some extent, Gatsby transforms himself from Jimmy Gatz to Jay Gatsby because he was unhappy with his parents: In his imagination, he "had never really accepted them as his parents at all" (p. 118). But to an even greater extent, Gatsby hears "the drums of his destiny" (p. 119) as defined by a version of the American dream of success that applies to men. In fact, whereas most young men, according to Nick, in moments of "intimate revelation," tell tales that are in reality "plagiaristic" (pp. 1–2), Gatsby goes a step further and actually lives out some of the myths of the culture.

In support of his new identity, Gatsby adopts what he believes are the appropriate mannerisms and surrounds himself with what he believes are the right props. He calls other men "Old Sport," drives an expensive, fancy car, and lives in a mansion in West Egg, which, he tells Daisy, he keeps " 'always full of interesting people, night and day. People who do interesting things. Celebrated people' " (p. 109). He also goes to great lengths to create a sense of authenticity. As Owl-Eyes puts it when he discovers that the books in Gatsby's library are real, " 'This fella's a regular Belasco. It's a triumph. What thoroughness! What realism!' " (p. 55).

Despite all his efforts, Gatsby's mannerisms and props often fail, in great part because his dream lacks a moral sense. For instance, Gatsby has made his fortune outside of the law. He also has no compunction about associating with Wolfsheim, the man who fixed the 1919 World Series and in so doing, in Nick's words, played "with the faith of fifty million people" (p. 88). As importantly, Gatsby's dream also lacks an aesthetic sense. The universe that he creates first in his imagination and then later and in reality in West Egg is one of "ineffable gaudiness," (p. 119), the beauty he commits himself to serving is "vast, vulgar, and meretricious" (p. 118). Moreover, at the parties at which he plays Trimalchio, his guests "conducted themselves according to the rules of behavior associated with amusement parks" (pp. 49–50).

For such reasons, Gatsby does not initially convince Nick that he was "the son of some wealthy people in the Middle West" (San Francisco, he tells Nick) who was "educated at Oxford, because, all my ancestors have been educated there for many years" (p. 78). Instead, when Gatsby first tells Nick his tale, Nick has to "restrain my incredulous laughter" because the "very phrases were worn so threadbare" (p. 79). Moments later, even though his incredulity has become fascination, Nick observes that listening to Gatsby "was like skimming hastily through a dozen magazines" (p. 80). In contrast, Daisy initially finds such pleasure in Gatsby's wealth that she ignores the gaudier realities. For instance, moved by Gatsby's display of expensive shirts, she sobs to him, " 'They're such beautiful shirts. . . . It makes me sad because I've never seen such – such beautiful shirts before' " (p. 112).

Nick in time suspends his doubts and puts his faith in Gatsby, whereas Daisy, concerned primarily with her own needs, first accepts Gatsby's persona and then, when it conflicts with those needs, turns away from it and from him. Tom, on the other hand, throughout the novel is skeptical about the role Gatsby plays. He scoffs at the notion that Gatsby went to Oxford, telling Nick and Jordan, " 'An Oxford man! . . . Like hell he is! He wears a pink suit" (p. 146). He also characterizes Gatsby as being " 'Mr. Nobody from Nowhere' " (p. 156), as someone who could only get " 'within a mile' " of Daisy by bringing " 'the groceries to the back door' " (p. 158), and as a " 'common swindler who'd have to steal the ring he put on her finger' " (p. 160).

Tom's reading of Gatsby is an accurate one. Gatsby's first mentor was Dan Cody, a "pioneer debauchee, who during one phase of American life brought back to the Eastern seaboard the savage violence of the frontier brothel and saloon" (p. 121). Moreover, even though Daisy was "the first 'nice' girl" Gatsby had ever known (p. 177), he "took what he could get, ravenously and unscrupulously – eventually he took Daisy one still October night" (p. 178), and he did so "under false pretenses" (p. 178).

Ironically, after he makes love to Daisy, Gatsby's attitude toward her changes, for "now he found that he had committed himself to the following of a grail" (p. 179). It is significant that Gatsby's commitment to Daisy is not merely the result of passion but rather one he makes deliberately, with the full knowledge that in so doing he will compromise his dream. Indeed, Gatsby equated kissing Daisy with embracing life's transiency, for he "knew that when he kissed this girl, and forever wed his unutterable visions to her *perishable* breath, his mind would never romp again like the mind of God" (p. 134; italics added).

Although Gatsby's fears are well founded, his acknowledgment of Daisy's mortality and his own is brief, for as he kisses her, he disregards what he knows and makes Daisy the embodiment of his dream. As Nick recounts it, "At his lips' touch she blossomed for him like a flower and the incarnation was complete" (p. 134).

In part, of course, Gatsby is drawn to Daisy because she already represents his dream to him, represents "the youth and mystery that wealth imprisons and preserves" (p. 179). In this regard, it is interesting to note that, in Nick's mind at least, it is Daisy's voice that holds Gatsby the most. Specifically, Nick defines her voice as being "a deathless song" (p. 116) of "inexhaustible charm" (p. 144), whereas it is Gatsby who identifies its distinctive quality, that it is " 'full of money' " (p. 144). But money and dreams are not enough to alter the reality of time's movement, for Daisy has created a life separate from Gatsby, a reality that Gatsby has difficulty accepting. For instance, when Daisy introduces Gatsby to her child, Nick observes, "Afterward he kept looking at the child with surprise. I don't think he had ever really believed in its existence before" (p. 140).

Gatsby's response to the changes that time has brought to Daisy's life is to try " 'to fix everything just the way it was before' " (p. 133). He wants Daisy to tell Tom that she had never loved him. He also wants "to go back to Louisville and be married from her house – just as if it were five years ago" (p. 133). By such actions, Nick believes, Gatsby hopes to "recover something, some idea of himself perhaps, that had gone into loving Daisy," for since Daisy married Tom, Gatsby's "life had been confused and disordered" (p. 133).

But ultimately Daisy cannot disregard the realities of her life, and so, when Gatsby insists that she tell Tom that she has "never loved him" (p. 159), Daisy breaks down. In a deeply emotional moment, she recognizes, perhaps for the first time, that her relationship with Gatsby is not merely a romantic gesture, not merely the playing out of an old fantasy, but an action that has serious consequences. In this moment, Nick describes her as looking at Jordan and him "with a sort of appeal, as though she realized at last what she was doing – and as though she had never, all along, intended doing anything at all" (p. 158). Nevertheless, Daisy tries to reconcile her life with Tom with her love for Gatsby. As Nick tells it, " 'Oh, you want too much!' she cried to Gatsby. 'I love you now – isn't that enough? I can't help what's past.' She began to sob helplessly. 'I did love him once – but I loved you too' " (p. 159).

In the hours that follow the scene in the Plaza Hotel, Daisy, at the wheel of Gatsby's car, runs over and kills Myrtle Wilson. She also fails to return to the scene of the accident. Gatsby, whose immediate thoughts are only with Daisy, makes the decision to help her avoid responsibility for her actions. In addition, worried about Tom's reactions to the episode in the Plaza, Gatsby waits outside the Buchanan home in case Daisy needs help, maintaining what Nick defines as a sacred vigil. Nick, on the other hand, understands that Daisy and Tom have restored some sort of intimacy. After looking in their window, he observes, "anybody would have said that they were conspiring together" (p. 175). In short, he recognizes that Daisy has betrayed Gatsby and that Gatsby's illusions have been shattered, that he now is "watching over nothing" (p. 175).

If, as Nick believes, Gatsby recognizes Daisy's betrayal, his awareness is sadly ironic. If Gatsby has come to terms with reality and let go of his dream, he is – for the first time since he began loving Daisy – facing life with all its pain. But Wilson, his own illusions about his marriage to Myrtle shattered, ends both Gatsby's life and his own.

In many ways, Daisy is like Gatsby. At crucial moments in her life, she deliberately chooses to embrace certain illusions and play certain roles as a way of creating for herself a sense of meaning and purpose and as a way of coping with "the pressure of the world outside" (p. 181). Restless because Gatsby is still in Europe with the army after World War I, Daisy becomes engaged to Tom because

> all the time something within her was crying for a decision. She wanted her life shaped now, immediately — and the decision must be made by some force — of love, of money, of unquestionable practicality — that was close at hand. (p. 181)

Daisy appears to have contained her feelings about leaving Gatsby for Tom. As far as Nick knows, she exhibits emotion only once, in a tearful and drunken episode the night before her wedding. It is as though her choice to marry Tom and to conform to the expectations of their social world has made her cynical. In short, even though Daisy's smile, like Gatsby's, reassures and her very presence promises excitement, she does not possess Gatsby's "extraordinary gift for hope" (p. 2). Perhaps for that reason she is more successful than Gatsby at playing roles and using gestures. For example, Nick dismisses the rumor that "Daisy's murmur was only to make people lean toward her" as "an irrelevant criticism that made it no less charming" (p. 11). And although Nick believes that Daisy's confession to him of her unhappiness was insincere and part of "a trick of some sort to exact a contributory emotion" from him (p. 21), yet once again, Daisy can instantly charm him "by opening up again in a flower-like way" (p. 24).

But it is Daisy's lack of purpose that most differentiates her from Gatsby (whose love for Daisy, in another irony, is what gives his life purpose). She and Jordan engage in talk that has "a bantering inconsequence" and "that was never quite chatter, that was as cool as their white dresses and their impersonal eyes in the absence of all desire" (p. 15). In several moments, Daisy's laments of boredom echo the voices in the "A Game of Chess" section of Eliot's *The Waste Land:* " 'What'll we do with ourselves this afternoon . . . and the day after that, and the next thirty years?' " (p. 141). But even in this frame of mind, Daisy more often than not poses. For instance, she tells Nick, " 'You see I think everything's terrible anyhow. . . . Everybody thinks so — the most advanced people. And I *know*. I've been everywhere and seen everything and done everything" (p. 21).

Daisy most reveals her ennui when she professes the hope that her daughter will be " 'a fool' " because " 'that's the best thing a girl can be in this world, a beautiful little fool' " (p. 21). The wish suggests Daisy's recognition of just how painful intelligence and consciousness can be. The context of her remark is also telling, for Daisy makes it within an hour of the child's birth, after she " 'woke up out of the ether with an utterly abandoned feeling' " because "Tom was God knows where' " (p. 21).

Eventually, because, as Jordan puts it, " 'Daisy ought to have something in her life' " (p. 96), she resumes her affair with Gatsby. But even though their relationship initially gives them and Nick the sense that "Ahead lay the scalloped ocean and the abounding blessed isles" (p. 141), it also disrupts Daisy's life. For example, when Gatsby joins Tom, Jordan, Nick, and Daisy for lunch at East Egg, Daisy becomes distressed. Being "on the verge of tears," and feeling that " 'it's so hot . . . and everything's so confused,' " she again wants to plan something. Just as when she married Tom, she hopes that taking some sort of action will allow her to mold "senselessness into forms" (p. 142).

The plan that the group devises – to rent a suite in the Plaza – does not bring the clarity or the order that Daisy seeks. Instead, the moment becomes charged with unhappy emotion. In the face of their confusion and heightened emotion, Daisy again chooses the course of action that she believes will bring her security: She turns to Tom. In so doing, she disregards what she has already painfully learned, that Tom, whose "sprees" she finds "revolting," has from the earliest months of their marriage failed her. Within hours, she makes a series of equally important, self-interested, and destructive choices. She does not return to the scene of the accident. Nor does she tell either the police or Tom that she was driving the car, an act of omission that eventually leads to Gatsby's death. She also does not call Gatsby the morning after the accident, does not attend his funeral, and does not send either a message or flowers.

The novel's subplots and supporting characters offer their own variations on the theme of individuals choosing illusions and playing roles as a way of creating a sense of meaning and order in their lives. Myrtle, for example, is driven by the version of the American dream that applies to women. Thus, although she believes, as Gatsby does, that success is measured in material possessions and a certain social role, like Daisy she assumes that those possessions and that role will be found in a relationship with a man who will be a provider, a caretaker, and, as she puts it, " 'a gentleman' " (p. 42).

Fitzgerald establishes the pattern almost immediately; Myrtle and Tom's New York apartment, decorated in a French motif, is a sign to Myrtle of social status, just as Gatsby's mansion on West Egg, "a factual imitation of some Hôtel de Ville in Normandy" (p. 6), symbolizes success to him. But as Gatsby's mansion with its blue lawn does not achieve the desired authenticity or elegance, so Myrtle and Tom's apartment is without grace: "The living-room was crowded to the doors with a set of tapestried furniture entirely too large for it, so that to move about was to stumble continually over scenes of ladies swinging in the gardens of Versailles" (p. 34).

In this setting, Myrtle adopts unattractive gestures and loses the "intense vitality that had been so remarkable" (p. 36) in West Egg. As Nick describes it:

> Her laughter, her gestures, her assertions became more violently affected moment by moment, and as she expanded the room grew smaller around her, until she seemed to be revolving on a noisy, creaking pivot through the smoky air. (p. 36)

Myrtle, like Gatsby, is ultimately the victim of illusions. Although she believes that she and Tom will marry, he clearly has no such intention. Indeed, Tom makes it clear that Myrtle's place in his life is tangential when they have a violent fight at their party over whether or not she should be allowed to say Daisy's name. When she insists on doing so, Tom breaks her nose.

Jordan, in contrast, knows which role is best for her to play and exactly how to play it. Nick finds this role attractive: As he puts it, "Almost any exhibition of complete self-sufficiency draws a stunned tribute from me" (p. 11). To sustain her role, however, Jordan avoids "clever, shrewd men" because, Nick believes, "she felt safer on a plane where any divergence from a code would be thought impossible" (p. 71). Jordan needs that sort of safety because she is "incurably dishonest" (p. 71), a trait that Nick excuses because he sees it as an appropriate coping device for a woman:

> She wasn't able to endure being at a disadvantage and, given this unwillingness, I suppose she had begun dealing in subterfuges when she was very young in order to keep that cool, insolent smile turned to the world and yet satisfy the demands of her hard, jaunty body. (p. 71)

In addition to lying, Jordan is often careless. When Nick accuses her of being a rotten driver, she justifies her own behavior on the grounds that other people are careful. When Nick warns her that she might meet " 'somebody just as careless as yourself,' " Jordan responds easily: " 'I hope I never will. . . . I hate careless people. That's why I like you' " (p. 72). But when Jordan become associated in Nick's mind with Daisy and Tom and the chaos and destruction they create, he moves away from the relationship. For her part, whatever her anger and disappointment, Jordan maintains her pose. And so, when Nick meets her for the last time, he notes, "She was dressed to play golf, and I remember thinking she looked like a good illustration" (p. 213). But even though Jordan is able to create a personality that is made up of a series of successful gestures, her life ultimately seems both purposeless and empty.

Tom Buchanan, like Jordan, lives according to a certain social code. For example, his code allows him extramarital affairs but denies them to Daisy. Tom is, however, careful to choose women who are not of his and Daisy's social class. When he and Myrtle go to New York together, he also defers "to the sensibilities of those East Eggers who might be on the train" by requiring Myrtle to sit "discreetly" in another car (p. 31). In Tom's mind, he is merely going off on a "spree." As he explains it, " 'I always come back, and in my heart I love [Daisy] all the time' " (p. 158).

Nick recognizes that Tom, like Daisy and Gatsby, found the most meaning and happiness in his past. As Nick explains it, Tom "had been one of the most powerful ends that ever played football at New Haven – a national figure in a way, one of those men who reach such an acute limited excellence at twenty-one that everything afterwards savors of anti-climax" (p. 7).[5] As an adult, Tom's life seems empty. After he tells Nick of his worries that the white race will lose its "control of things" to other races, Nick thinks, "Something was making him nibble at the edge of stale ideas as if his sturdy physical egotism no longer nourished his peremptory heart" (p. 25). In a sense, Tom is a case of arrested adolescence. Even after the tragedies of the novel, Nick sees Tom as being childlike, as being someone who makes messes that others have to clean up (p. 216).

Nick's choices, perhaps even more than those of the other characters, are affected by his sense of vulnerability, on the one hand, and his desire for order, on the other. Throughout the novel, his narrative is dominated by his ambivalence about whether it is better to embrace life's possibilities or to try to escape from its uncertainties and dangers. And so, although events lead Nick to be increasingly wary of change and to yearn for a world that is "in uniform and at a sort of moral attention forever," he continues to celebrate Gatsby's "romantic readiness" and his "extraordinary gift for hope" (p. 2).

Initially, Nick not only finds change exciting, he tends to couch his reactions in universal terms. For example, when he describes commuters returning home to West Egg in twilight, he thinks, "It was the hour of a profound human change, and excitement was generating on the air" (p. 115). When he watches "the great bursts of leaves growing on the trees," he reveals, "I had that familiar conviction that life was beginning over again with the summer" (p. 5). Jordan too seems to share Nick's sentiments when, later in the novel, she rebukes Daisy for being "morbid" and tells her, " 'Life starts all over again when it gets crisp in the fall' " (p. 142).

Nick also recognizes that he "began to like New York, the racy, adventurous feel of it at night, and the satisfaction that the constant flicker of men and women and machines gives to the restless eye" (p. 69). In addition, he finds pleasure in the rich fantasy life that New York offers:

> I liked to walk up Fifth Avenue and pick out romantic women from the crowd and imagine that in a few minutes I was going to enter into their lives, and no one would ever know or disapprove. Some-

times, in my mind, I followed them to their apartments on the corners of hidden streets, and they turned and smiled back at me before they faded through a door into warm darkness. (p. 69)

Nick is unquestionably drawn to Daisy and Gatsby because each offers him a similar sense of life's promise and, not incidentally, of his own worth as well. He is attracted to the "promise" in Daisy's voice "that she had done gay, exciting things just a while since and that there were gay, exciting things hovering in the next hour" (p. 11). He finds her voice "thrilling," perhaps because, like life itself, it seems to be "an arrangement of notes that will never be played again" (p. 11). Daisy's smile is equally appealing because it makes Nick believe "that there was no one in the world she so much wanted to see" (p. 11). Nick is attracted to Gatsby for similar reasons. He sees "something gorgeous about him, some heightened sensitivity to the promises of life. . . . it was an extraordinary gift for hope, a romantic readiness such as I have never found in any other person and which it is not likely I shall ever find again" (pp. 2–3). Moveover, in Gatsby's smile, as in Daisy's and in the smiles of the women about whom he fantasizes, Nick finds a sense of his own value:

> It was one of those rare smiles with a quality of eternal reassurance in it, that you may come across four or five times in life. It faced – or seemed to face – the whole external world for an instant, and then concentrated on *you* with an irresistible prejudice in your favor. It understood you just as far as you wanted to be understood, believed in you as you would like to believe in yourself, and assured you that it had precisely the impression of you that, at your best, you hoped to convey. (p. 58)

There are, nevertheless, many moments in which Nick feels alienated from the world around him. Sometimes he deliberately chooses that stance. For example, on the opening page of the novel, he acknowledges that he has always been uncomfortable with too much intimacy, recalling that he has frequently "feigned sleep, preoccupation, or a hostile levity" in the face of "intimate revelations." At other times, he regrets his stance of being "without," believing that, by such distance, he is wasting life itself. Once again, in a passage that echoes *The Waste Land*, Nick extends his own feelings to others:

At the enchanted metropolitan twilight I felt a haunting loneliness sometimes, and felt it in others — poor young clerks who loitered in front of windows waiting until it was time for a solitary restaurant dinner — young clerks in the dusk, wasting the most poignant moments of night and life. (p. 69)

In such moments of discontent, Nick especially seems to need a sense of order. After his experiences during World War I, he decides that "instead of being the warm centre of the world, the Middle West now seemed like the ragged edge of the universe." His response to such feelings of disorientation are to choose the path that "everybody I knew" had chosen: moving to New York and entering the bond business (p. 3). The choice is without risk, for both his aunts and uncles concur with it, and his father agrees to support him for a year.

Nick, however, becomes increasingly unsettled as events force him to move beyond thoughts about life's promise and bring him face to face with its harsher realities. For example, when he learns of Tom's affair with Myrtle, he feels "confused and a little disgusted" (p. 25). He also assumes that Daisy will share his reaction, observing, "It seemed to me that the thing for Daisy to do was to rush out of the house, child in arms" (p. 25). When Myrtle's sister tells him that Daisy won't give Tom a divorce because she is Catholic, Nick is "a little shocked at the elaborateness of the lie" (p. 40). And when Daisy attends one of Gatsby's parties for the first time, Nick sees it through her eyes and feels "an unpleasantness in the air, a pervading harshness that hadn't been there before" (p. 126).

After the scene in the Plaza, when Daisy, Gatsby, and Tom display such raw emotion, Nick reacts even more intensely. Now he is explicit that he sees change as being not exciting but dangerous. Shed of his own illusions about Gatsby's past and also about Daisy's ability to be worthy of Gatsby's dream, Nick remembers that the day marks his thirtieth birthday and thinks, "Before me stretched the portentous, menacing road of a new decade" (p. 163).

Such negative feelings prompt Nick to decide that "human sympathy has its limits" (p. 163). As Tom drives Nick and Jordan back to East Egg, Nick feels remote from Tom and from his heightened emotions. For the moment at least, he turns to Jordan, who, "unlike Daisy, was too wise ever to carry well-forgotten dreams from age to age" (p. 163). He also continues to think of the future as threatening, not exciting. In his mind, the only promise he finds in his birthday is "the promise of a decade of loneliness, a thinning list of single men to know, a thinning brief-case of enthusiasm, thinning hair" (p. 163).

Nick's premonitions about the dangers and the loneliness of the future prove apt. Within a day, Daisy has killed Myrtle Wilson in a hit-and-run accident; George Wilson — led by Tom to believe that Gatsby had been driving "the death car" — has murdered Gatsby and then killed himself; and Nick has become estranged from his friends. In fact, after the accident, "Feeling a little sick" and wanting to be alone, Nick refuses Jordan's invitation to come into the Buchanan's house, thinking, "I'd be damned if I'd go in; I'd had enough of all of them for one day, and suddenly that included Jordan too" (p. 171). Tom and Daisy's actions after the accident are especially offensive to Nick. Aware that their carelessness and their refusal, both individually and together, to assume responsibility for their actions and their relationships have led to the deaths, his indictment is severe:

> It was all very careless and confused. They were careless people, Tom and Daisy — they smashed up things and creatures and then retreated back into their money or their vast carelessness, or whatever it was that kept them together, and let other people clean up the mess they had made. . . . (p. 216)

The night of Myrtle's death, Nick cannot sleep because, as he tells it, "I tossed half-sick between grotesque reality and savage, frightening dreams" (p. 176). In other words, neither reality unadorned by illusion nor illusion itself offers an escape from feelings of vulnerability. Soon, however, Nick decides that it is the East that is "haunted" for him, "distorted beyond my eyes' power of correction" (p. 213). In his mind, West Egg is especially disturbing. It remains in his "more fantastic dreams" as "a night scene by El Greco" — "grotesque, crouching under a sullen, overhanging sky and a lustreless moon" (p. 212) in which wealth is irrelevant in the face of the lack of order and caring.

To escape this world where reality is grotesque and where even nature is not nurturing but threatening, Nick decides to go home again. Disregarding his feelings about the East's "superiority" to the Midwest and ignoring his sense that the Midwest is a place of "bored, sprawling, swollen towns beyond the Ohio, with their interminable inquisitions which spared only the children and the very old" (p. 212), Nick decides to return home. Not unexpectedly, his need for order persists. Even though he has come to think that he may be "half in love" (p. 214) with Jordan, he ends their relationship because he "wanted to leave things in order and not just trust that obliging and indifferent sea to sweep my refuse away" (p. 213). Nick is also explicit that he no longer wants complexity or to be a "well-rounded man" (p. 5); instead, he has decided that "life is much more successfully looked at from a single window after all" (p. 5).

In other words, like Gatsby and Daisy, Nick makes a deliberate decision to embrace his past even though he knows that such a choice is itself based on illusions and romantic memories of childhood. Remembering those moments, particularly the train rides when he returned home from prep school and believed that he and his friends were "unutterably aware of our identity with this country," Nick elaborates:

> That's my Middle West — not the wheat or the prairies or the lost Swede towns, but the thrilling returning trains of my youth, and the street lamps and sleigh bells in the frosty dark and the shadows of holly wreaths thrown by lighted windows on the snow. I am a part of that. . . . (pp. 211–12)

Nick once again thinks of his own choices in universal terms. As he reflects on the events of the novel, he looks out on Long Island Sound and imagines the vision "that flowered once for Dutch sailors' eyes" (p. 217). That flowering, he knows, like Daisy's, existed only "for a transitory enchanted moment" (p. 217) before it, too, gave way to reality. He also knows that the reality itself was shaped by the attempt of individuals like Gatsby to translate their dream into material terms, but whose flaw, like Gatsby's, was that they too served a "vast, vulgar, and meretricious beauty" (p. 118) that devastated "the fresh green breast of the new world" (p. 217).

Nick's view that America has destroyed its dream in the attempt to make that dream a reality contributes to his belief that the vision of the Dutch sailors brought humanity "face to face for the last time in history with something commensurate to [their] capacity for wonder" (pp. 217–18). But even as Nick seems resigned to that loss of hope, he continues to yearn for it, perhaps as much as he yearns for a sense of order. Even though he knows that neither Gatsby's dream nor Daisy – as the incarnation of that dream – is worthy of Gatsby's capacity for wonder, he remains in awe of "the colossal vitality of [Gatsby's] illusion" (p. 116). As he explains after the fact:

> It had gone beyond her, beyond everything. He had thrown himself into it with a creative passion, adding to it all the time, decking it out with every bright feather that drifted his way. No amount of freshness can challenge what a man will store up in his ghostly heart. (p. 97)

Eventually, Nick shifts his focus from Gatsby to a more universal one and allies Gatsby's lost dream to America's dream and to his own. Moreover, both Nick's words and his actions, especially his final reverie about Gatsby and his decision to return to the Midwest, underscore his understanding of just how compelling illusions rooted in the past can be and, at the same time, just how destructive it is for individuals to try to locate meaning in those illusions. As he says about Gatsby:

> He had come a long way to this blue lawn, and his dream must have seemed so close that he could hardly fail to grasp it. He did not know that it was already behind him, somewhere back in that vast obscurity beyond the city, where the dark fields of the republic rolled on under the night.
>
> Gatsby believed in the green light, the orgiastic future that year by year recedes before us. It eluded us then, but that's no matter – tomorrow we will run faster, stretch out our arms farther. . . . And one fine morning –
>
> So we beat on, boats against the current, borne back ceaselessly into the past. (p. 182)

Ultimately, Nick takes away from his experience in West Egg what he seems to believe is also the lesson of the American experience: that moments of hope and promise and wonder can be found only in the past, that – except in the imagination – the past is irrecoverable, that the present brings with it only the betrayal of dreams, and that the conscious individual must nevertheless continue to hope and to struggle.

The dilemma that Nick, Daisy, and Gatsby face is, of course, a human one as well as an American one: whether to embrace the dreams of youth and keep alive the hopes bred in innocence or to face the reality that such dreams are inevitably elusive and illusory because they are part of the past. In the end, of course, as the novel demonstrates, neither the choice of embracing illusions nor the effort to live without them suffices. And in that light, the best path for the conscious individual seems in fact to be that which Fitzgerald outlined a decade later in *The Crack-Up*: that such an individual must try to function in the face of "the contradictions between the dead hand of the past and the high intentions of the future" and, at the same time, accept the paradox inherent in doing so.

NOTES

1 F. Scott Fitzgerald, "The Crack-Up," *The Crack-Up*, ed. Edmund Wilson (New York: New Directions, 1945), p. 69.
2 Ibid., p. 70.
3 F. Scott Fitzgerald, *The Crack-Up*, p. 78.
4 Fitzgerald, of course, is not alone among modern writers to explore these concerns; quite the contrary. The question of how to live in the face of time's movement is age-old, and the more modern dilemma of how to find meaning in a world that seems to have become a moral and spiritual wasteland informs much of twentieth-century fiction. But what makes Fitzgerald's treatment of such questions in *The Great Gatsby* especially interesting is that, unlike many modern novelists, he does not offer action, social responsibility, consciousness, or even art itself as an appropriate response (in this regard, it is interesting to note that the only character in the novel with artistic aspirations is the ineffectual photographer, Mr. McKee.) Nor does Fitzgerald create existential heroes who perform acts of social responsibility or who find happiness and self-definition in consciousness itself. He also does not create characters who cope with time and the modern world by confronting death directly, seeking meaning in nature, or retreating altogether from the world of time, events, and the human community through suicide, madness, or exile.

77

5 In *The Crack-Up*, Fitzgerald reveals that one of his own "juvenile re-grets" was "not being big enough (or good enough) to play football in college." Unlike Tom Buchanan, however, Fitzgerald as an adult rele-gated such fantasies to the level of "childish waking dreams" (p. 70).

5

The Great Gatsby
and the Great American Novel

KENNETH E. EBLE

1

IN length, the book barely qualifies as a full-sized novel. In sub-ject, it is about an American bootlegger who nourishes an ado-lescent dream about a golden girl he can't have. Its plot does little more than tell us who the protagonist is and get him killed off in the end by the down-and-out husband of the blowsy mistress of the rich brute who has married the girl whom the hero wants but can't have. Its manner of telling is disjointed, albeit by the literary design of the author, and accompanied by some seemingly casual moralizing by an omnipresent narrator sounding suspiciously like the author and sort of occupying himself at other times by taking an interest in a woman golfer who cheats, the only other substan-tial character in the novel if we except a denizen of the under-world, the mistress's dog and friends, Gatsby's father, a bunch of assorted party goers, and one mourner.

From this perspective, the adulation *The Great Gatsby* has re-ceived may seem totally out of proportion. For half a century, it has held a high place among twentieth-century novels. Its numer-ous reprintings around the world and its successive presentations on film have made Gatsby as identifiable an American figure as Huck Finn. It has revived the twenties, set current fashions, and provided dialogue for three generations of devoted readers. In these respects alone, the question of its literary merits set aside, it qualifies as a great American novel. For clearly, it has added a name to that relatively small number of factual and fictional Americans by which Americans know themselves and are known by the world. And it has done so by means of a writer's craft working within the traditional form of a long fictional narrative. If a substantial claim is to be made for *The Great Gatsby* as the great American novel, it will have to be made by a more considered examination. What I propose here is to examine the novel's relationship to the concept of the "great American novel"; the substance of the novel, its "great argument," as Edith Wharton phrased it; and the novel's structure and style, its excellence as a *literary* work, a *novel*.

John William De Forest, less than a great novelist himself, raised the question of "the great American novel" in an essay with that specific title in 1868.[1] The literary nationalism that spawned the concept had already been expressing itself for at least half a century and had resulted in such documents as Joel Barlow's *Columbiad*, Royall Tyler's *The Contrast*, and Emerson's "The American Scholar." The novels that De Forest could measure the concept against were not a promising lot. Their authors are largely forgotten by now – Paulding, Brown, Kennedy, and Simms: "ghosts," who "wrote about ghosts, and the ghosts have vanished utterly." Melville escaped De Forest's attention, much as *Moby-Dick*, for all its bulk, escaped most critics' notice until the twentieth century. Hawthorne's *The Scarlet Letter* was there to be considered, but De Forest found the novel, as others did also, too insubstantial, too provincial, to be either novel enough or American enough to qualify. The novel he did single out was *Uncle Tom's Cabin*, which had a sufficiently broad, true, and sympathetic representation of American life to make it worth considering. De Forest was biased here by his own understandable preoccupation with the Civil War and its aftermath, although *Uncle Tom's Cabin* deserves more attention than it gets. Edmund Wilson has pointed out: "It is a much more impressive work than one has ever been allowed to suspect. The first thing that strikes one about it is a certain eruptive force."[2]

By the time Fitzgerald began to write, seekers after the great American novel had a much wider choice, and since then a still wider choice. Edith Wharton's essay, "The Great American Novel," in the *Yale Review* in 1927, expressed skepticism toward the very idea. As far as she could determine, "The great American novel must always be about Main Street, geographically, socially, and intellectually." This was a restriction she did not accept, and most of her essay is about the limitations such insistence places on the novelist. Moreover, what might be expected of American novelists when Main Street, she argued, offered "so meagre a material to the imagination?" Still, she pointed out Robert Grant's *Unleavened Bread*, Frank Norris's *McTeague*, and David Graham Phillips' *Susan Lenox* as not only "great American novels," but great novels.[3]

Fifty years later, Philip Roth, writing *The Great American Novel* in name if not in fact, offered *The Scarlet Letter, Moby-Dick, Huckleberry Finn, The Ambassadors*, and *The Golden Bowl* as possibilities. To be precise, these are the choices of a "Vassar slit," presumably schooled by a modern American English department and badgered into responding to Roth's fictional Hemingway roaring: "'What about *Red Badge of Courage!* What about *Winesburg, Ohio! The Last of the Mohicans! Sister Carrie! McTeague! My Antonia! The Rise of Silas Lapham! Two Years Before the Mast! Ethan Frome! Barren Ground!* What about Booth Tarkington and Sara Orne Jewett, while you're at it? What about our minor poet Francis Scott Fitzwhat'shis name? What about Wolfe and Dos and Faulkner?'"[4]

Roth has Hemingway decide, "'It hasn't been written yet,'" and to his boast that he will write it, a seagull croaks, "Nevermore." Perhaps gulls, if not Poe, have the last word on this matter. Frank Norris said something similar about the time Fitzgerald was born: "The Great American Novel is not extinct like the Dodo, but mythical like the Hipogriff." He also said that the great American novelist was either "as extinct as the Dodo or as far in the future as the practical aeroplane," which suggests that there should be dozens of them around today. Norris had many things to say about the novel, favoring novels that were "true" and with "a purpose," and embracing both "realism" and "romance." He surmised that in his time, the great American novel must be "sectional," and yet he foresaw a unified America and American novelists reaching a "universal substratum" common to all men. By such a route, he had to admit, the idea of a distinctively "American" novel disappears when a great novelist sounds "the world-note."[5]

In his fiction — and it is well to note that he was christened Benjamin Franklin Norris, — Norris moved to the novel of epic scope that many others have in mind as requisite to the great American novel. He saw the settling of the American West as "the last great epic event in the history of civilization,"[6] as Fitzgerald also implied in *The Great Gatsby*. In this respect, Whitman had already written the great American novel, although technically it happened to be a poem, *Leaves of Grass*, rather than a novel. Whitman, as well as anyone in prose or in poetry, defined this underlying ambition for the great American novel.

The preface to the 1855 edition of *Leaves of Grass* begins with two whopping assertions, the second scarcely more defensible than the first: "The Americans of all nations at any time upon the earth have probably the fullest poetical nature. The United States themselves are essentially the greatest poem."[7] The elaboration of these assertions, the emphasis on "the largeness of nature or the nation" needing "gigantic and generous treatment," are too familiar to need repeating. Fitzgerald expressed his awareness of Whitman's impact in an essay published in 1926 and noted for its bringing Ernest Hemingway to public attention, "How to Waste Material: A Note on My Generation": "Ever since Irving's preoccupation with the necessity for an American background, for some square miles of cleared territory on which colorful variants might presently arise, the question of material has hampered the American writer. For one Dreiser who made a single-minded and irreproachable choice there have been a dozen like Henry James who have stupid-got with worry over the matter, and yet another dozen who, blinded by the fading tale of Walt Whitman's comet, have botched their books by the insincere compulsion to write 'significantly' about America."[8]

Fitzgerald's judgment of Dreiser and James aside, his awareness of the force of Whitman's message is directly related to the idea of the great American novel and what that novel should be about. His essay describes various attempts and failures to deal with "American" materials. He cites the treatment of the American farmer, of American youth, of "American politics, business, society, science, racial problems." His point is that this search for and exploitation of American material is largely in vain: "One author goes to a midland farm for three months to obtain material for an epic of the American husbandman! Another sets off on a like errand to the Blue Ridge Mountains, a third departs with a Corona for the West Indies — one is justified in the belief that what they get hold of will weigh no more than the journalistic loot brought back by Richard Harding Davis and John Fox, Jr., twenty years ago."[9]

Fitzgerald had already made these points in various parodies of popular novels and, more directly, in a letter to Maxwell Perkins just after *The Great Gatsby* was published.[10] The letter was about Thomas Boyd's new novel, *Samuel Drummond*, which Perkins had described to Fitzgerald in terms of high praise. To Fitzgerald the novel sounded "utterly lowsy," and he sketched out a "History of the Simple Inarticulate Farmer and his Hired Man Christy" to make his point. The basic issue he raises is the same as the one in his essay: the essential weakness of novels dealing quaintly and falsely with American materials — in this instance, the earthy struggle between the American farmer and the soil — to satisfy some kind of craving for the great American novel. In both of these statements, Fitzgerald did not cite his own example from the recent past, the fact that *This Side of Paradise*, if it did not speak for all of America, was still received by the public (and promoted by Fitzgerald) as speaking for American youth. *The Beautiful and Damned*, which followed in 1922, might justifiably have been regarded as trying to take in all parts of Fitzgerald's longer list, beginning with "business" and ending with "literature."

The Great Gatsby, as Fitzgerald perceived in writing it, was something different, something more consistent with and closer to Fitzgerald's wish reported by Edmund Wilson: "I want to be one of the greatest writers who have ever lived, don't you?"[11] One cannot understand Fitzgerald's work, can't come to terms with the possibility of *The Great Gatsby* being the great American novel, without responding to the naiveté, the presumptuousness, the grandiosity of that remark — as naive and presumptuous and grandiose as Whitman talking about the poetic natures of an American nation and its poets.

That sense of measuring himself against great writers persisted throughout Fitzgerald's life. The curriculum he set up for Sheilah Graham in 1939[12] was both a recapitulation of his own reading and a considered judgment of what books would best serve

Sheilah Graham's beginning and his own continuing education. The novels form a diverse and respectable list, weighted toward the modern, as one might expect, and as much European as British and American. Among the various novels or parts of novels are most of those necessary to serious study of the nineteenth- and twentieth-century novel: *The Red and the Black, Vanity Fair, Bleak House, The Brothers Karamazov, Anna Karenina* and *War and Peace, Eugénie Grandet, Madame Bovary, Sister Carrie, Man's Fate,* a half-dozen or so novels by Henry James, a similar number by Hardy, Joyce's *Portrait of the Artist,* Faulkner's *Sanctuary,* and others. He prized his meeting with Joyce in 1928 and pasted the letter he received from him in his copy of *Ulysses.* The drunken serenading with which he and Ring Lardner paid their respects to Joseph Conrad is also a part of Fitzgerald lore. But there is a seriousness in this reading and literary hero worshiping that underscores Fitzgerald's conception of himself as a serious novelist. The long struggle to bring another novel into being after completing *The Great Gatsby* is not entirely to be blamed on the conditions of Fitzgerald's personal life. In part, the struggle was forced on Fitzgerald because of his ambitions to go beyond *The Great Gatsby,* to achieve that writer's goal he set forth in a letter to Scottie, "so that the thing you have to say and the way of saying it blend as one matter – as indissolubly as if they were conceived together."[13] Fitzgerald's letters to Scottie are further testimony to his seriousness as a writer. The reading he sets forth for her reaches back to *Moll Flanders* and forward to Thomas Mann's *Death in Venice.* "I wish now," he wrote to her June 12, 1940, "I'd *never* relaxed or looked back – but said at the end of *The Great Gatsby:* 'I've found my line – from now on this comes first. This is my immediate duty – without this I am nothing.'"[14]

But what Fitzgerald did not emphasize, either in an offhand remark or in his written comments, was his being an American writer, a fashioner of American materials, a writer of the great American novel. To put it in a simple form, he solved the problem of what he should use for material by setting the problem aside. More precisely, he recognized that a preoccupation with what a novel should be about was probably a strike against the novel at the outset. Thus, he became free to deal as best he could with that

84

limited substance he had, free and inadvertently American to "spin my thread from my own bowels," as Emerson said, or in Whitman's words, "launch forth, filament, filament, filament, out of itself, ever unreeling them." Or, in Fitzgerald's matter-of-fact words, "My God! It was my material, and it was all I had to deal with."[15]

What I am suggesting here is that if there is such a thing as the great American novel, it will not be because of the American-ness of what it is about. Such a novel may be, as *Moby-Dick* is, about whaling and whales and those who pursue them, much of which is American because the author is American, or as *Huckleberry Finn* is American by the same line of reasoning, or as *The Great Gatsby* is. Thus, Fitzgerald's novel is animated by and makes its impact through a writer's intensely devoted attempt to understand a portion of human experience, the personal dimensions of that experience that reach into the hearts of human beings and the contexts that always complicate and alter such personal responses. From one perspective, these contexts are indubitably American, as much so as they seem to convey the pulse beat of the urban American 1920s. But from another, they are no more American than Ithaca is Greek or Bleak House British. What is kept before the reader — and not setting aside the particulars by which that is made manifest — are the longings for love, wealth, power, status, for dreaming and realizing dreams and facing the realities of which dreams are compounded and by which they are compromised.

There is another side to this observation. The story of *The Great Gatsby*, both to its advantage and its disadvantage in weighing the novel's merit, is intertwined for many readers with the story of F. Scott and Zelda Fitzgerald. If one result is to question the likelihood of such a person as Fitzgerald being able to write a great novel, another is to endow the novel with something of the authenticity of the *real* story of the Fitzgeralds' gaudy but tragic lives. I further suggest that this preoccupation with "self," the fictional one focused on Gatsby, the real one lying behind the fascination that the Fitzgerald story continues to have for the American public, may be what is more American about the novel than any other aspect. Benjamin Franklin's *Autobiography* may be the original American novel, even though, like *Leaves of Grass*, it is not a novel.

That aside, what followed the *Autobiography* was a succession of great American books – poems, essays, romances, novels – that were chiefly explorations of the self. Emerson's *Essays* and Thoreau's *Walden* can be added to the novels already mentioned, and to those, *Hopalong Cassidy*, on whose fly leaf Gatsby had set down his own Franklinesque resolves.

The Great Gatsby, then, is in the right American line, in regard to conceptions, implied and stated, about what should constitute the great American novel. More directly, of course, *Gatsby*, despite its brevity, illuminates the American past and present, answers the challenge of getting within its pages something of the scope and variety and dynamics of American life, the light and dark of American experience, the underside and upperside of American society. Moreover, it does so within the larger framework of human experience, invariably moving readers to the dimensions of myth that convey meaning independent of time, place, and the particulars of experience.

Robert Ornstein's "Scott Fitzgerald's Fable of East and West" is one of dozens of essays that explore the novel's symbolism, allusions, ironies, ambiguities, and mythical dimensions. Ornstein argues that Fitzgerald has created "a myth with the imaginative sweep of America's historical adventure across an untamed continent. . . . One can even say that in *The Great Gatsby* Fitzgerald adumbrated the coming tragedy of a nation grown decadent without achieving maturity." His essay, however, refuses to narrow the theme of the novel to that of the betrayal of the American dream; rather, its theme "is the unending quest after the romantic dream, which is forever betrayed in fact and yet redeemed in men's minds." Ornstein sees this theme brought out not only in terms of American experience but also in an embodiment of the romantic response to life. "Gatsby *is* great," he writes, "because his dream, however naive, gaudy, and unattainable, is one of the grand illusions of the race, which keep men from becoming too old or too wise or too cynical of their human limitations."[16] Fitzgerald dramatized that perception in a brilliant way in "Absolution," originally intended as an introduction to the Gatsby story. There the crazed priest tells the young boy: "'Go and see an amusement park. . . . It's a thing like a fair, only much more glittering. . . . But don't get up close, because if you do you'll only feel the heat and the sweat and the life.' "[17] One of the prominent themes in *The Great Gatsby* is that familiar one, "All that glitters is not gold," and its corollary, "but it glitters, all the same." For much of the world and for America itself, America has been the great amusement park, holding its World's Fairs and World Series and awarding "World Championships" as events in which most of the world never participates. What better setting for a meditation on the romantic vision and romantic disillusionment?

This dimension of *The Great Gatsby* has held a central place in the criticism of the novel since the first revival of interest in Fitzgerald shortly after his death. Prior to that time, Fitzgerald seems justified in replying to John Peale Bishop's letter about the novel: "It is about the only criticism that the book has had which has been intelligible, save a letter from Mrs. Wharton,"[18] or to Edmund Wilson: Not one of the reviews "had the slightest idea what the book was about."[19] When it was praised by such writers as T. S. Eliot, Edith Wharton, and Gertrude Stein, it was in such general terms as Eliot's "the first step that American fiction has taken since Henry James."[20] Even to such a sympathetic critic as Fitzgerald's contemporary Paul Rosenfeld, the novel was "beautifully done, breezy throughout. . . . extraordinarily American, like ice cream soda with arsenic flavoring, or jazzmusic in a fever-dream."[21] Only Thomas Caldecott Chubb, writing in the *Forum* in 1925, perceived the book to be "a fable in the form of a realistic novel." "At once a tragedy and an extraordinarily convincing love tale and an extravaganza."[22]

Notwithstanding the restrained and ambivalent responses to the novel when it first appeared, most of the later criticism has been searching and favorable. John W. Bicknell begins with a hint dropped by Lionel Trilling that Fitzgerald's novel is a prose version of Eliot's *The Waste Land*, a poem Fitzgerald knew almost by heart. Like Conrad, Fitzgerald sees "the modern corruption in contrast to a lost rather than to an emergent ideal." Bicknell's overall critical intent is to determine whether *Gatsby* is tragic or merely pessimistic. He ends by accepting Alfred Kazin's view that "in a land of promise 'failure' will always be a classic theme." Marius Bewley's essay, "Scott Fitzgerald's Criticism of America,"[24] finds more to praise in *Gatsby*, perhaps because he does not assume that tragedy is the definitive measure of a novel's greatness. He writes: "Fitzgerald – at least in this one book – is in line with the greatest masters of American prose. *The Great Gatsby* embodies a criticism of American experience – not of manners, but of a basic historic attitude to life – more radical than anything in James's own assessment of the deficiencies of his country. The theme of *Gatsby* is the withering of the American dream." Bewley's essay acknowledges that "Gatsby, the 'mythic' embodiment of the American dream, is shown to us in all his immature romanticism. His insecure grasp of social and human values, his lack of critical intelligence and self-knowledge, his blindness to the pitfalls that surround him in American society, his compulsive optimism, are realized in the text with rare assurance and understanding. And yet the very grounding of these deficiencies is Gatsby's goodness and faith in life, his compelling desire to realize all the possibilities of existence." Edwin Fussell's "Fitzgerald's Brave New World" also mentions the universality as well as the uniqueness of the American experience. "After exploring his materials to their limits, Fitzgerald knew, at his greatest moments, that he had discovered a universal pattern of desire and belief and behavior and that in it was compounded the imaginative history of modern, especially American, civilization."[25]

With respect to its serious import, its examination of both American life and lives in much of the modern Western world, *Gatsby* bears comparison with those other books that might stand as the great American novel. It does not sprawl like *Moby-Dick*, nor hover and ruminate like *The Scarlet Letter*, nor heap up its substance like any work of Dreiser. It does not hint and suggest and qualify like Henry James, nor does it have the robust, yet lyric, quality of *Huckleberry Finn*. Yet, consider some vital qualities all these novels share. Chiefly these are *Gatsby*'s moral preoccupations, as inseparable from the novel as from *Moby-Dick* or *The Scarlet Letter*, and its dramatization of innocence coming into experience, as memorably fixed in Nick Carraway and Gatsby as in Huck and Jim or Ishmael on the *Pequod*. Moreover, with the final page of the novel establishing "the old island here that flowered once for Dutch sailors' eyes" (p. 217), Fitzgerald gives the novel an amplitude that bears comparison with James's powers in *The Ambassadors* or *The American*. The persuasiveness of Fitzgerald's prose (or Keats's poetry) aside, that moment of gazing on the "fresh, green breast of the new world" must have been and may be, even "for the last time in history," "something commensurate to his capacity for wonder" (pp. 217–18).

The events following the twenties, notably a worldwide economic depression and the outbreak of another world war, may unknowingly have attuned modern readers to the serious dimensions of *Gatsby*. For it has been since World War II, and particularly in America, that the realities of living in a world of limited resources have begun to register. Throughout much of its history, America was a place of endless expanding and advancing. Without exaggerating greatly, one can place *Gatsby* with those classic statements that recall us to the fact that, as Fitzgerald came to recognize, one cannot both spend and have. Projected beyond the personal, one cannot espouse infinite progress but must accept some kind of eternal return, "boats against the current, borne back ceaselessly into the past" (p. 218).

2

All readers have been affected by Fitzgerald's style, for Fitzgerald was marvelously sensitive to the sounds and cadences of language. "For awhile after you quit Keats," he wrote, "all other poetry seems to be only whistling or humming."[26] His attraction to Conrad was due to Conrad's attention to the power of the written word, to "an unremitting never-discouraged care for the shape and ring of sentences" that aspired to "the magic suggestiveness of music – which is the art of arts."[27] Fitzgerald's sentences have movement, grace, clarity, directness when necessary, force when desired, and cadences appropriate to the mood or emotion or scene. Matched with the visual images, simile and metaphor, sentences like this emerge in profusion: "We drove over to Fifth Avenue, so warm and soft, almost pastoral, on the summer Sunday afternoon that I wouldn't have been surprised to see a great flock of white sheep turn the corner" (p. 33). "Yet high over the city our line of yellow windows must have contributed their share of human secrecy to the casual watcher in the darkening streets, and I was him too, looking up and wondering. I was within and without, simultaneously enchanted and repelled by the inexhaustible variety of life" (p. 43). "For a while these reveries provided an outlet for his imagination; they were a satisfactory hint of the unreality of reality, a promise that the rock of the world was founded securely on a fairy's wing" (p. 119). Fitzgerald's style is remarkably apt and precise, even when he is dealing with nearly ineffable matters: "He was a Son of God – a phrase which, if it means anything, means just that – and he must be about His Father's business, the service of a vast, vulgar, and meretricious beauty" (p. 118). Part of that aptness is the quality of Fitzgerald's wit, apparent in that Homeric catalog of guests that begins: "From East Egg, then, came the Chester Beckers and the Leeches, and a man named Bunsen, whom I knew at Yale, and Doctor Webster Civet . . . " and ends "All these people came to Gatsby's house in the summer" (pp. 73–6). Or the bite of such a description as: "the dim enlargement of Mrs. Wilson's mother which hovered like an ectoplasm on the wall" (p. 36).

These quotations, chosen to exemplify Fitzgerald's style, serve also to illustrate the inseparability of style and content. Major and minor characters in *Gatsby* are brilliantly created by both what Fitzgerald chooses to reveal about them and how he reveals it. Most of the preceding passages are important in creating a character and shaping a reader's perception of that character. In the first instance, that pastoral touch, seemingly a stylistic flourish, is exactly right for perceiving Tom Buchanan and Myrtle in contrast to the ash heaps surrounding Wilson's garage and the tacky apartment where Tom has been keeping her. Similarly, Nick Carraway's reflection calls a reader's attention to his being both inside and outside the main action, a vital aspect of his characterization. And speaking of Gatsby as a son of God who goes about his Father's business reverberates powerfully in one's accumulating impressions of that central character. The minor characters in the novel are created with that terse exactness that is apparent in Fitzgerald's handling of words in the novel: Meyer Wolfsheim and his human molar cufflinks; Mr. McKee, who has "'done some nice things out on Long Island'" (p. 38); George Wilson, veiled in ashen dust; and Owl-Eyes, finding real books in Gatsby's library, but with the pages uncut.

"I think it is an honest book," Fitzgerald wrote in the introduction to the Modern Library Edition in 1934, "that is to say, that one used none of one's virtuosity to get an effect, and, to boast again, one soft-pedalled the emotional side to avoid the tears leaking from the socket of the left eye, or the large false face peering around the corner of a character's head."[28] It is this restraint, even more than the virtuosity of effects, that distinguishes Fitzgerald's style in *The Great Gatsby*. In almost all of his other fiction, the quality of the prose gives otherwise ordinary materials a polish that not only exacted high prices from popular magazines but may have hinted at more profundity than the content delivered. In *Gatsby*, straining for effect is seldom apparent. The whole novel is compactly put together, as much by repetition of images and symbols as by exposition and narrative.

The opulence associated with both Gatsby and the Buchanans is established in Chapter 1 by a physical description of the Buchanans' house and lawn: "The lawn started at the beach and ran toward the front door for a quarter of a mile, jumping over sun-dials and brick walks and burning gardens – finally when it reached the house drifting up the side in bright vines as though from the momentum of its run" (p. 8). At the end of the first chapter, the cadences change as we see Gatsby on his lawn at night: "The wind had blown off, leaving a loud, bright night, with wings beating in the trees and a persistent organ sound as the full bellows of the earth blew the frogs full of life. The silhouette of a moving cat wavered across the moonlight, and turning my head to watch it, I saw that I was not alone – fifty feet away a figure had emerged from the shadow of my neighbor's mansion and was standing with his hands in his pockets regarding the silver pepper of the stars" (p. 25). A paragraph later, Chapter 1 ends with the "single green light" (p. 26) at the end of the dock that became one of the final images in the novel. Between those two images are other descriptions of landscape and house, from the "blue gardens" after "the earth lurches away from the sun" (pp. 47–9) to the "sharp line where my ragged lawn ended and the darker, well-kept expanse of his began" (p. 99) in Chapter 5. At the end, these images accumulate: the opening of the windows at dawn, the photograph of the house that Gatsby's father shows to Nick, "cracked in the corners and dirty with many hands" (p. 207), and Carraway's last look at "that huge incoherent failure of a house. On the white steps an obscene word, scrawled by some boy with a piece of brick, stood out clearly in the moonlight, and I erased it, drawing my shoe raspingly along the stone" (p. 217).

James Joyce said of *Ulysses* that he had put in enough enigmas and puzzles to keep professors busy for centuries. *The Great Gatsby* lacks that density, but it has engaged the attention of many professors to date. Color symbolism, patterns of images, sources and analogues, ambiguities, mythical dimensions continue to be worked over. Passages of dialogue are as carefully wrought as descriptive passages. Some have become passwords of *Gatsby* cultists: "'Can't repeat the past? . . . Why of course you can!'" (p. 133) and "'Her voice is full of money'" (p. 144) and "'In any case . . . it was just personal'" (p. 182). Others are equally part of the texture of the novel, shaping character, amplifying meanings, knitting parts together: "'Is it a boy or a girl?'" Myrtle asks of the "gray old man who bore an absurd resemblance to John D. Rockefeller." "'That dog? That dog's a boy.' 'It's a bitch,' said Tom decisively. 'Here's your money. Go and buy ten more dogs with it'" (pp. 32–3). Fitzgerald also knew when to have his characters stop talking. In the draft of the novel, much of Gatsby's story is told in dialogue as he talks to Nick. It permits him to talk too much, to say, for example, before Fitzgerald excised it: "'Jay Gatsby!' he cried suddenly in a ringing voice. 'There goes the great Jay Gatsby. That's what people are going to say – wait and see.'"[29]

As with details of his style, the structure of *The Great Gatsby* has been subject to minute examination, Fitzgerald's debt to Conrad was early pointed out: "for the use of style or language to reflect theme; for the use of the modified first person narration; for the use of deliberate 'confusion' by the re-ordering of the chronology of events." Fitzgerald's use of "a series of scenes dramatizing the important events of the story and connected by brief passages of interpretation and summary" is like Henry James's "scenic method."[30] In these respects and others, *The Great Gatsby* responds, as a great American novel surely should, to the call for "newness" sounded repeatedly throughout America's literary history.

I have written at length elsewhere, as have others, about the structure of *The Great Gatsby*[31] and will not go into detail here. The facsimile of the manuscript enables any reader to study Fitzgerald's revisions, small and large. He was a careful reviser, nowhere in his work more than in *The Great Gatsby*.

In general, his revisions were devoted to solving the technical problems of presenting the story – the narrative structure – and in sharpening, trimming, amplifying descriptions, narrative, dialogue. The choice of Nick Carraway as narrator was probably not made until some jelling of the essential story took place in Fitzgerald's mind. The short stories "Absolution" and "Winter Dreams" are written in the conventional third person. The longer form in itself may have raised questions about the mode of telling; the examples of James and Conrad were at hand to suggest the use of a first-person narrator. Although that choice was in one sense a technical one, it was also a means of presenting his material "through the personal history of a young American provincial whose moral intelligence is the proper source of our understanding and whose career, in the passage from innocence to revaluation, dramatizes the possibility and mode of a moral sanction in contemporary America."[32] Such a view still seems fairly to describe Fitzgerald's intent, although a spate of criticism has pointed out the unreliability of Carraway as a narrator. The choice of narrator was related to other technical problems, chiefly that of how and when (and in what order and way in the novel) the narrator uncovers for the reader the complete story of Gatsby's past. Like other modern novels, *Gatsby* does not follow a straightforward chronology; Fitzgerald worked hard to preserve the advantages of a disjointed structure against the confusion such a method may create. One of the effects was to keep Gatsby from fully materializing, helping Fitzgerald solve the difficult problem of making a deliberately shadowy figure the central character of the novel.

It is not easy to summarize even the most important changes Fitzgerald made to achieve the structure he wanted. Suffice to say that changes and shifts of materials kept Gatsby offstage for a longer period of time than in the first version. Between his first appearance as a figure on his lawn and Nick's conversation with him in Chapter 4, the reader is exposed to Daisy, Tom, Jordan Baker, and the Wilsons, is transported through the valley of ashes and into Myrtle's Manhattan apartment, and gets a fuller glimpse of Gatsby during the first party at his house. The chief results, aside from heightening one's interest in the mysterious Gatsby, are the various juxtapositions of beauty and squalor, peace and violence, vitality and decay – in short, the intensifying of the central contrasts between the ideal and the real.

All this is accomplished in three chapters, with the material that originally comprised these chapters being rearranged in various ways. Chapter 4 extends our acquaintance with Gatsby, and Chapter 5 becomes the center of the novel. This chapter was very closely reworked, chiefly in order to give it a static quality, to approximate in the telling Gatsby's attempt to make time stand still. From that chapter on, the novel picks up speed. The real world intrudes in the guise of a reporter through whom details of Gatsby's actual past are exposed. A second party, sharper delineation of Tom Buchanan, and the second trip into Manhattan prepare the reader for the final sweep of the plot to the running down of Myrtle Wilson, "her left breast . . . swinging loose like a flap" (p. 165). "I *want* Myrtle Wilson's breast ripped off," he wrote Maxwell Perkins. "It's exactly the thing, I think, and I don't want to chop up good scenes by too much tinkering."[33]

The remaining chapters were chiefly reworked to wind down events with economy but also with measured impact. Some of Gatsby's explanations were shifted to the present tense to give them greater immediacy. The last chapter shifted attention to Nick, but still kept him linked tightly to Gatsby by means of the funeral, his talk with Gatsby's father, and those benedictory words pronounced by Owl-Eyes, "'The poor son of a bitch'" (p. 211). Nick's last encounter with Tom underscores Fitzgerald's achievement of making Carraway a vital character in his own right, a technical device that helps hold the structure together, a means of amplifying the moral and social dimensions of the novel and the way in which the story gets told. The last image of the book, the "fresh, green breast of the new world," was originally written as the conclusion of the first chapter. Now placed at the end of the novel, it enlarges even as it brings the novel to an end.

This discussion of style and structure argues for the novel's high degree of finish, surely a merit in a novel, although not necessarily what many would associate with the great American novel. The exchange between Fitzgerald and Thomas Wolfe illustrates my point. Wolfe, a great "putter-inner" of a novelist, challenges Fitzgerald's criticism of his work by citing Shakespeare, Cervantes, and Dostoevsky as "great putter-inners — greater putter-inners, in fact, than taker-outers and will be remembered for what they put in . . . as long as Monsieur Flaubert will be remembered for what he left out."[34] Wolfe's arguments are unanswerable for those who insist that a great American novel must *"boil* and *pour."* By that measure, *The Great Gatsby* must fall short, for all that it has a size beyond its actual page length.

Still, one can, only half facetiously, propose that *Gatsby* is an *efficient* novel, and thereby identifiably and pleasingly American. For the time one puts into it, a great deal comes out. Even its nuances of style are not likely to be lost on American readers, for they have the laconic power of sarcasm, the brevity of the one-liner, and the directness of American speech. Its moral dimensions still touch the sense of decency and fair play, without engaging the reader in time-consuming ethical and metaphysical speculations. The novel's topicality is that of the twenties, but is not confined to that decade. The author's rhetorical flourishes are nicely spaced; the story has some action and plenty of pathos shading off into tragedy. It raises basic questions citizens of a democracy have to wrestle with: How does one recognize greatness without an established social order? How does the acquisition of power, wealth, and status accord with the professions of democratic equality? How does an idealist and an individual — both prized qualities of the American — keep himself from succumbing to the materialism of the masses or from kicking himself loose from the universe? If all this can be accomplished in a book under 200 pages and still selling for under $10 (it was priced at $2 in 1925), what could be greater and more American than that?

3

The foregoing claims may be the strongest that can be made for the stature of *The Great Gatsby* as the great American novel. A less convincing form of reasoning, but one worth addressing briefly, is to see *Gatsby* in the line of American novels of manners, novels like those of Howells and James and Edith Wharton. It is Wharton, in the essay previously mentioned, who points out that "Traditional society, with its old-established distinctions of class, its passwords, exclusions, delicate shades of language and behavior, is one of man's oldest works of art."[35] She expresses dismay that American novelists have been turned away from this material, from the novel of manners, just as James expressed to Howells his dismay that American society didn't furnish the richness and diversity that would support such novels. Nevertheless, Frank Norris saw in Howells that breadth of vision and intimate knowledge of Americans East and West that went part way toward establishing an "American school of fiction."[36] If he did not quite claim that Howells was writing the great American novel, he did call attention to Howells's efforts to establish the novel of manners as an estimable kind of American fiction.

The novel of manners in Howells's hands and in Fitzgerald's did not preclude its being a serious and socially engaged work. Gertrude Stein's letter in response to *The Great Gatsby* recognized that Fitzgerald was "creating the contemporary world much as Thackeray did his in *Pendennis* and *Vanity Fair* and this isn't a bad compliment."[37] Howells's and Fitzgerald's examinations of American society show the novel of manner's concern for moral behavior measured against social norms. In the background of both authors' work are reminders of that moralistic and idealistic strain of Americans who populated a wilderness and created its Washingtons and Lincolns. But the society each saw around him was one in which that kind of American was hard pressed to withstand the amoral and materialistic drive for power that characterized American success. The tragic hero set forth in *Gatsby* is really the American failure, failing to hold to the course of power that wins success and failing, moreover, because of the strength of idealistic illusions.

Too few readers know Howells's *The Landlord at Lion's Head*, a novel that started out as one merely about a "jay" student at Harvard but that became one of Howells's strongest social novels. Jeff Durgin, the protagonist of the story, is one more provincial who is sufficiently strong and amoral, like Gatsby, to gain power and wealth by his own shrewdness and drive and luck. *Landlord* lacks the tightness and finish of *Gatsby*, but in its central theme it may be more modern and less sentimental than Fitzgerald's novel. For Durgin and his dream are not defeated, much as the many Gatsbys who pursue their driving materialistic dreams are not defeated in American life. Rather, Durgin's success at the end of that novel is the American success of power and money. The girl of Durgin's dreams turns out to be so sanctimonious as to deserve little better than the pallid artist who claims her and who, like Carraway in *Gatsby*, provides the novel's supposed moral center. Durgin ends up with the daughter of a Europeanized mother and a wealthy American father, a woman all but a dolt would prefer to Durgin's earlier choice. Like Tom Buchanan and Daisy, the Durgins seem likely to make it in the modern world, although Carraway says that they have "retreated back into their money or their vast carelessness" (p. 216) and he back to pondering his father's wisdom that "a sense of the fundamental decencies is parcelled out unequally at birth" (p. 2). A generation or two earlier than Fitzgerald, Howells, too, saw what the American dream was for most citizens: money, power, social position, and a modicum of culture. Only a "provincial squeamishness" (p. 216) in both writers caused them to question the substantiality and rightness of the materialistic dream.

I am not arguing that the novel of manners somehow provides its writers with some special claim to a novel's greatness. In fact, probably the opposite is true in regard to American writers. Mark Twain's condemnation of Jane Austen's work conveys the disrespect that assigns such novels to a distinct and lesser category. The point is, rather, that the novel of manners has an appropriateness to American writing fully as much as does the romance or tall tale. Howells and James both extended that form, achieving at their best something of what Dickens and Thackeray achieved for the British novel. Balzac and Zola can also fit into this category, as can Norris and Fitzgerald.

But categorizing a novelist's work is a folly not unlike looking for the great American novel. It matters little whether *The Great Gatsby* is the great American novel or not. It probably matters that writers, much less readers, keep such concepts before them. No reader needs an unrelieved diet of great novels, American or any other kind. Writers, on the other hand, probably do need the urging of tradition, the example of other writers and other novels and kinds of novels, and the idea of greater books than they have yet written. Even then, the novels they write will be as various as the lives they live and the thoughts they think. As there are many American writers and readers, so there are bound to be many American novels, some of them great.

Howells looked back on his career and wrote: "Mostly I suppose I have cut rather inferior window glass with it . . . perhaps hereafter when my din is done, if any one is curious to know what the noise was, it will be found to have proceeded from a small insect which was scraping about on the surface of our life and trying to get into its meaning for the sake of the other insects, larger and smaller. That is, such has been my unconscious work, consciously, I was always, as I still am, trying to fashion a piece of literature out of the life next at hand."[38] It may be enough to say of *The Great Gatsby* that F. Scott Fitzgerald achieved what he set out to do, to write "something *new*, something extraordinary and beautiful and simple + intricately patterned."[39]

NOTES

1 John William De Forest, "The Great American Novel," *The Nation* 6 (1868):27–9.

2 Edmund Wilson, *Patriotic Gore: Studies in the Literature of the American Civil War* (New York: Oxford University Press, 1962), p. 5.

3 Edith Wharton, "The Great American Novel," *Yale Review* 16 (July 1927):646–56.

4 Philip Roth, *The Great American Novel* (New York: Holt, Rinehart and Winston, 1973), p. 33.

5 Frank Norris, *The Responsibilities of the Novelist and Other Literary Essays* (Westport, Conn: Greenwood Press, 1968), pp. 85–9.

6 Ibid., p. 61.

7 Walt Whitman, *Leaves of Grass: Comprehensive Reader's Edition*, ed. Harold W. Blodgett and Sculley Bradley (New York: New York University Press, 1965), p. 709.

8 F. Scott Fitzgerald, "How to Waste Material — A Note on My Generation," *The Bookman* 63 (May 1926):262–5.

9 Ibid., 263.

10 *The Letters of F. Scott Fitzgerald*, ed. Andrew Turnbull (New York: Scribners, 1963), pp. 183–8.

11 Edmund Wilson, "Thoughts on Being Bibliographed," *The Princeton University Library Chronicle* 5 (February 1944):54.

12 Sheilah Graham, *College of One* (New York: Viking Press, 1967), pp. 204–21.

13 Turnbull, ed., *Letters*, p. 11.

14 Ibid., p. 79.

15 F. Scott Fitzgerald, Introduction to *The Great Gatsby* (New York: Modern Library, 1934), p. x.

16 Robert Ornstein, "Scott Fitzgerald's Fable of East and West," *College English* 18 (December 1956):139, 143.

17 F. Scott Fitzgerald, "Absolution," *The Stories of F. Scott Fitzgerald: A Selection of 28 Stories*, with an Introduction by Malcolm Cowley (New York: Scribners, 1951), p. 171.

18 Turnbull, ed., *Letters*, p. 358.

19 Ibid., p. 342.

20 *The Great Gatsby: A Study*, ed. Frederick J. Hoffman (New York: Scribners, 1962), p. 179.

21 *Correspondence of F. Scott Fitzgerald*, ed. Matthew J. Bruccoli and Margaret Duggan (New York: Random House, 1980), p. 171.

22 *F. Scott Fitzgerald: In His Own Time*, ed. Matthew J. Bruccoli and Margaret Duggan (Kent, Ohio: Kent State University Press, 1971): A remarkably good collection of Fitzgerald materials, including reviews of *The Great Gatsby* at the time of publication. See also G. Thomas Tanselle and Jackson R. Bryer, "*The Great Gatsby* — A Study in Literary Reputation," *Profile of F. Scott Fitzgerald*, ed. Matthew J. Bruccoli (Columbus, Ohio: Merrill, 1971), pp. 74–91.

23 John W. Bicknell, "The Waste Land of F. Scott Fitzgerald," in *F. Scott Fitzgerald: A Collection of Criticism*, ed. Kenneth Eble (New York: McGraw-Hill, 1973), pp. 67–80.

24 Tanselle and Bryer, *The Great Gatsby: A Study*, pp. 263–85.

25 Ibid., pp. 244–62.

26 Turnbull, ed., *Letters*, p. 88.

27 Joseph Conrad, "Preface to *The Nigger of the Narcissus*," in Tanselle and Bryer, *The Great Gatsby: A Study*, pp. 59–64.
28 Fitzgerald, Introduction to *The Great Gatsby*, p. x.
29 F. Scott Fitzgerald, *A Facsimile of the Manuscript*, ed. Matthew J. Bruccoli (Washington, D.C.: Bruccoli Clark/Microcard, 1973), p. xxix.
30 James E. Miller, Jr., *The Fictional Technique of Scott Fitzgerald* (The Hague: Martinus Nijhoff, 1957), pp. 79–81.
31 Kenneth E. Eble, "The Craft of Revision: *The Great Gatsby*," *American Literature* 26 (November 1964):315–26.
32 Thomas Hanzo, "The Theme and the Narrator of 'The Great Gatsby,'" *Modern Fiction Studies* 2 (Winter 1956–7):190.
33 Turnbull, ed., *Letters*, p. 175.
34 F. Scott Fitzgerald, *The Crack-Up*, ed. Edmund Wilson (New York: New Directions, 1945), p. 314.
35 Wharton, "The Great American Novel," 652.
36 Norris, *Responsibilities of the Novelist*, pp. 193–200.
37 Fitzgerald, *The Crack-Up*, p. 308.
38 *Life in Letters of William Dean Howells*, ed. Mildred Howells, vol. II (Garden City, N.Y.: Doubleday, 1928), pp. 172–3.
39 Bruccoli and Duggan, *Correspondence*, p. 112.

6

Fire and Freshness: A Matter of Style in *The Great Gatsby*

GEORGE GARRETT

I have never yet known, or, indeed known of, a contemporary
American writer who did not admire *The Great Gatsby*. This
evidence, admittedly and purely anecdotal, is, also in my experience, unique. I know of no other twentieth-century masterpiece in
our language or, for that matter, in our Western tradition about
which this can be said. Let it be said again as simply as possible: I
have never known an American writer, of my generation or of the
older and younger generations, who has not placed *Gatsby* among
the rare unarguable masterpieces of our times. In some cases this
admiration is frankly surprising, because *Gatsby* seems to be, in
form and content, so different from what has otherwise engaged
the passions and commitment of one writer and the other. It really
has not seemed to matter very much which side of the (aesthetic)
tracks the writer came from or what side of the street the writer is
working. In an era of increasingly specialized special interests, it
does not seem to be a matter defined or limited by race, creed,
color, gender, or country of national origin. And strangely, in an
age when we have become so politicized that even the toothpaste
one uses becomes, like it or not, a political statement, writers of all
political stripes and persuasions seem to admire *Gatsby*, even as,
inevitably, they describe the characters and the story in somewhat
different terms.

Finally, it doesn't even seem to matter very much if the writer in
question holds any positive feelings about the life and (other)
works of F. Scott Fitzgerald. Many did not admire him in his
lifetime – although it is clear that he was much envied from time
to time. Many do not have feelings one way or the other, nothing
beyond a polite shrug, even now. But *Gatsby* itself stands by itself –
a permanent monument of our literature, a national treasure. And

I share the consensual wisdom, although not without a willingness to question it, if only to ask where it comes from. In part perversely, because I have always been automatically contemptuous of trends and fashions, especially *intellectual* trends, which seem to be a contradiction in terms (like the concept of military justice), I have always preferred *Tender Is the Night.* It was always my favorite among the Fitzgerald novels, since I read them, back to back, for the first time, to the best of my recollection, in the summer of 1948 in Princeton. *Gatsby* was assigned reading in a summer school course, the first time Fitzgerald was ever read at Princeton as part of an official course. It was, in fact, the first time at Princeton that any American writers beyond the life and times of Henry James were allowed to be part of the authorized academic curriculum. The course was new and different, a departure. It was an altogether stunning, unforgettable experience to "discover" William Faulkner (*The Sound and the Fury*) and Ernest Hemingway (*The Sun Also Rises*) in that summer. But it was very heaven to be in Princeton reading *The Great Gatsby*, as a class assignment, and then finding, in the stacks of the brand new Firestone Library, the stories and *This Side of Paradise* and *Tender Is the Night* and the others. And over at the U-Store you could buy, and I did, *The Last Tycoon* and *The Crack-Up*, edited by Edmund Wilson.

All of us that summer planned to be the next F. Scott Fitzgerald. We have all come a distance, a far piece, since then, swept by waves of unimaginable change, until, surfacing nearly a half century later, it seems that almost everything has changed beyond memory or repair. One of the things that has not changed, however, that still shines with authentic inner light, is *Gatsby.* That it has this same glowing effect on writers young enough to be my sons and daughters, new enough not to care a serious hoot about Old Nassau, I find an absolutely fascinating phenomenon.

To a certain extent, it may be a matter of historical content and the long, attractive shadows of nostalgia, but that cannot explain the depth of the novel's lasting appeal. Much of the context and content is lost now in the present. Clearly, only a modest handful of American writers and critics alive now, of any age (and forget the foreigners, even the English, who haven't a real clue), possess by birth, education, and experience the assumed knowledge and the imagination to understand the very subtle social implications and ambiguities that lie at the center, the very heart, of the story of *Gatsby*. Even at the time, the delicacy of Fitzgerald's sensitive recording of a specific and special world, as envisioned and judged by a particular and special intelligence, Nick Carraway, must have escaped many of his contemporaries. Significantly, the letters about *Gatsby* he savored from prominent writers he admired — for example, the letters from Gertrude Stein, Edith Wharton, and T. S. Eliot — stress and praise aspects of form as much as content. Each differently, they see *Gatsby* as advancing the art of the novel not so much from what it talks about as in the interesting ways and means of its making. As for us, it is very hard now to unlearn all that has happened since 1925; difficult, if not impossible, to imagine ourselves safely on the other side of the Great Depression and World War II and all the wars since then.

In one respect, then, contemporary interest in and excitement about the subjects and content of *Gatsby* derive from its odd prescience. Ash heap and eyeglasses, sordid orgy and casual accident, murder and suicide, lust and unrequited love — these are literary signs we have come to live among as if they had always been there, inherent in any conventional literary picture of modern American life. There is, in fact, a direct line of influence and authority running from *Gatsby* to a great many of our most prominent contemporary literary artists, both popular and serious. The signs and portents of Joan Didion, for example, or of Renata Adler, are rooted in Fitzgerald's acres of ashes in *Gatsby*, as are the economic minimalism of Raymond Carver, the half-stoned nihilism that pervades the stories of Ann Beattie, the lyrical ambiance of the novels and stories of Richard Yates. Gore Vidal, not deeply sympathetic to Fitzgerald, is nevertheless clearly admiring of the "small but perfect operation" of *Gatsby*. Of all these, and so many others, by the way, only the quirky Vidal has the depth and subtlety, rooted in old American experience, to understand some of what was eccentric and original about *Gatsby*. At any rate, American writers of all stripes and stamps, from Marxists to reactionaries, seem to be at home with the apparent content of *Gatsby*, to believe in its world, to take it for granted.

It is worth remembering that the down side of the Jazz Age,

namely, the Depression, was several years beyond the horizon in 1925 and that the main line of action in the story of *Gatsby*, the summer of 1922, was firmly set in the booming post–World War I years. Worth keeping in mind that prophets of doom seemed more outrageous and eccentric then than they would a decade later. It is part of Tom Buchanan's foolishness that he sees doom and trouble ahead. Worth recalling that popular fiction in which crimes could be allowed to go without punishment (if only by fate and bad luck) was very rare. After all, in American films and television, as late as the 1960s there was a serious problem of getting Code approval for a story in which vice was not punished in some way. It was startling in 1925 to let the Buchanans off the hook with a brief judgmental aside by the narrator: "They were careless people, Tom and Daisy — they smashed up things and creatures and then retreated back into their money or their vast carelessness, or whatever it was that kept them together, and let other people clean up the mess they had made" (p. 216). That they have done what they have done and can walk away from it safely and cheerfully enough, with nobody but the reader and the narrator any the wiser, was as daring as it was remarkable.

There are other things, qualities of which our own ignorance and lack of imagination now deprive us. There is so much drinking in *Gatsby*, and, of course, Fitzgerald was such a heavy drinker at times (and we know all about that now), that it is tricky to keep in mind the fact that both the story and the telling of it are deep in the heart of Prohibition. Which was, as a constitutional amendment, very much the law of the land. And which was not yet, either by Fitzgerald or others, seen as coming to an easy end either soon or painlessly. Time has turned the underworld and internecine wars, the blood and savagery that accompanied Prohibition, into something close to comedy, perhaps musical comedy. But Fitzgerald knew very well the shock value he gained by having so much drinking in his novel. (As did Hemingway in *The Sun Also Rises*, although that story was conveniently set in Europe.) It is significant that Jay Gatsby and Daisy Buchanan meet again, tentative and a little shy at first, in the proper atmosphere of an intimate and wonderfully awkward little tea party at Carraway's cottage. And, in accuracy and fairness, we have to recognize that, daring as he was, Fitzgerald carefully demonstrates throughout the book the bad results that inevitably follow from excessive drinking. Jay Gatsby is self-disciplined and abstemious; this is a rhetorical plus. The fact that Daisy does not drink is viewed ambiguously, more a matter of "an absolutely perfect reputation" (p. 93) than, perhaps, a sign of virtue.

Just so, adulterous affairs and, indeed, even premarital sex were still to be viewed as essentially criminal vices in polite society; and, to an extent, the views of polite society were confirmed by the law. Tom's affair with Myrtle (and the fact that she would dare to call him at home!), together with the absence of any apparently serious consequences, to himself at least, coming from it were conceived as shocking elements in the novel. Tom's promiscuity is rhetorically presented, and so intended to be taken, as wickedness rather than a "problem" or a bad habit. Gatsby's lifetime obsession with the image and reality of Daisy may be more than a little crazy and more than a little vulgar in its material manifestations – the extraordinary house, the parties, the fancy yellow car, and the piles of gorgeous shirts over which Daisy wept; but his dedication to her (including even the folly of asking "too much" (pp. 133, 159) of Daisy, asking her to confess that she had never loved anyone else but him) and his love for her were morally solid and appropriate for their time. Knowing better, even knowing why he was doing it, Gatsby had been Daisy's lover. "He took what he could get, ravenously and unscrupulously – eventually he took Daisy one still October night, took her because he had no real right to touch her hand" (p. 178). After which – "He felt married to her, that was all" (p. 179) – he always wanted to do the right thing. Buchanan, from a good family and background, has criminal vices. Gatsby, although a technical criminal of sorts and a man who mingles with strange and exotic types – the mysterious Jew Wolfsheim, show business types, flotsam and jetsam of society – possesses the best American middle-class standards of the time.

Only a few can still believe, still fewer remember, that there was a time not so long ago when celebrity of any kind, even the kind of celebrity Fitzgerald himself had acquired by the time he came to write *Gatsby*, had a chilling effect upon one's social position. The "best people" never appeared in the press except, perhaps, on the occasion of a wedding or funeral. The "best people" did not, beyond the wild-oats days of youth, mingle with celebrities and show business types, famous opera stars sometimes excepted. It is not quite true that American society despised the lively arts, but it is certainly true that most artists of all kinds, even those from good family, were somewhat suspect and a little bit déclassé. The Homeric list of Gatsby's guests from East Egg and West Egg is monumental in its witty snobbery. And as for Jews (the sinister and shady, two-dimensional Wolfsheim) or ethnics (the pathetic Henry C. Gatz, Gatsby's father, "a solemn old man, very helpless and dismayed, bundled up in a long cheap ulster against the warm September day" [p. 200]), these are not people one might have met except on some most unusual occasion or in the pages of a novel. To understand the prevalent attitude toward the very idea or image of the Jew at that time, one can take quite seriously the stance of Eliot in his early poems. Or one can turn to Edith Wharton's letter of congratulations in which she asserts, "it's enough to make this reader happy to have met your *perfect* Jew, & the limp Wilson, & assisted at that seedy orgy in the Buchanan flat, with the dazed puppy looking on."[1] The truth is, as both Fitzgerald and Edith Wharton knew (both in Europe at the time), the nineteenth century had not yet ended, socially at least, in America. For a moment of almost surreal social topsy-turvy, consider Nick's celebrated drive with Jay Gatsby into New York, over the Queensboro Bridge:

> A dead man passed us in a hearse heaped with blooms, followed by two carriages with drawn blinds, and by more cheerful carriages for friends. The friends looked out at us with the tragic eyes and short upper lips of southeastern Europe, and I was glad that the sight of Gatsby's splendid car was included in their sombre holiday. As we crossed Blackwell's Island a limousine passed us, driven by a white chauffeur, in which sat three modish negroes, two bucks and a girl. I laughed aloud as the yolks of their eyeballs rolled toward us in haughty rivalry. (pp. 82–3)

No comment is necessary. Except, perhaps, to point out that the language, and the reactions of the narrator and the anticipated reader, were not only neutral but decently appropriate for the time. Which was almost the last time they would be so in serious

American literature. Popular narrative was (to an extent remains) slow to change and follow. Perhaps it should be noted, however, that the *author's* intention in this brief sight gag was clearly to show Carraway's modernity, his openness to and delight in the otherwise shocking (to the reader) confusions of order in America.

All of this is stated only to make the point that in many ways we are far removed, as Americans, and as writers and readers as well, from the content and context of *Gatsby*. The old social guidelines have vanished.

If it is hard for us to imagine and to reconstruct the world Fitzgerald wrote about and out of, it is only fair to remind ourselves that, some extraordinary prescience aside, our world was beyond his imagining as well. He could not, for example, possibly have conceived of a time when this novel's art might be submitted to the scrutiny and judgment of literary critics and historians, preservers of the totems of the American tribe, who might themselves be ethnic or Jewish or black. That is to say, even as he felt the end of something and sensed many changes, Fitzgerald could not imagine the end of society as he knew it, except by an apocalypse.

In stressing what might be called the societal inaccessibility of *The Great Gatsby* to the contemporary reader, there is another social note worth mentioning. It happens to be something Nick Carraway mentions to us, a point *he* wants to make. Although there are fine-tuned differences and distinctions among all of the principals, there is one common bond. They are one and all outsiders. As Carraway points out in the final chapter: "I see now that this has been a story of the West, after all — Tom and Gatsby, Daisy and Jordan and I, were all Westerners, and perhaps we possessed some deficiency in common which made us subtly unadaptable to Eastern life" (p. 212). That remark, like many others made by Carraway, is layered in irony, more than a little ambiguous. But it does carefully call to mind, in case anyone had missed the fact, that nobody at all from the *real* society of the East even appears in this story. Some of the dregs of that society do, indeed, show up at Gatsby's parties; but in truth the whole story is a playing out, on foreign territory as it were, as alien and exotic as the France and Spain of *The Sun Also Rises*, of a story of love and death among expatriates.

I think it can be convincingly argued that we are by now far removed, imaginatively and in fact, from at least the *rhetorical social world of Gatsby*. And a case can be made, persuasively I believe, that precisely because Fitzgerald was so sensitively attuned to that world, and because that world was created and dramatized through the words and consciousness of a single character, Nick Carraway, we are no more likely to find out what Fitzgerald "really felt" about that world, from the text, than we are ever likely to know the views of our language's preeminent anonymous artist. That is, we know much about Elizabethan attitudes and prejudices, and we know much of this from the plays of Shakespeare. But we know precious little about what Shakespeare felt or thought, if anything, *except as an Elizabethan*. In some ways the world of *Gatsby*, although deceptively tricked out with things we know of and can believe in, is as foreign to us as Elizabethan and Jacobean England. And yet there stands this particular novel, by acclamation taken as nearly perfect in all detail, by example taken by writers, and thus readers, as admirable and enormously influential. If it is not really a matter of content or context, then it is, I believe, a matter of form that makes it so. Finally it is, then, a matter of style, an imperishable style, that has made *Gatsby* a permanent experience.

Briefer than it seems to be – for there are any number of adroitly used literary devices in *Gatsby* that are associated with a much more leisurely, old-fashioned kind of storytelling, giving a serious impression of much more abundance than is, in truth, the case – *Gatsby* is also much more complex in its method of presentation than the luminous clarity of its language implies. Most of the critics have taken due note of the influence of Joseph Conrad on the novel's strategy, particularly insofar as the story is filtered through the consciousness of an alert and sensitive first-person narrator who stands as a witness to the main thrust of the central action even as he works out a knotty story, with its particular and pressing problems, of his own. Carraway's story of that summer is important to himself. He loses in the game of love, turns thirty, loses, too, in his choice of work and place to be, and by the end (which is in fact the beginning of the telling of this story) has turned his back on all that and gone home for good. Yet the main thing that happens to Carraway, from the reader's point of view, is his fascination and involvement with his neighbor – Gatsby. The character of Carraway, as he presents himself, is complex and not entirely relevant to the subject of style. But it needs to be noted that he is an ambiguous character, one about whom the reader is intended to have mixed feelings; that these mixed, sometimes distinctly contradictory feelings give him more weight and solidity as a character than most witness–narrators; that these mixed feelings add more suspense and mystery to the elements of the story he relates and the ways he chooses to relate them.

However, to deal, in partial abstraction, with the matter of form and style, it is necessary to simplify, perhaps to oversimplify, what is naturally complex. All first-person narratives are presumed, by inference at the very least, to be either directly told to us, that is, spoken, or written; in the latter case, shaped into the form of a manuscript. "Heart of Darkness" is a story presumed to be told aloud to a small group of witnesses (including the original narrator) on a becalmed boat waiting for the tide to turn. "The Turn of the Screw," on the other hand, presents a speaking narrator who kindly allows us to read a written manuscript (written by somebody else) over his shoulder. Both of these effects, although equally strong in original authenticity, as is the case of any good first-person story, at least at its beginning, are also oddly and deliberately distanced from the events that make up the story. That is to say, by definition, from the beginning and for as long as the narrator is both engaging and apparently trustworthy, the principal action (event) of any given first-person story is the telling of the story itself. That is all that is really presumed to be happening – a story is being told. Sometimes it is written; sometimes it is spoken; sometimes, for the sake of celebrating the spoken vernacular, it is, as in *Huckleberry Finn*, assumed to be dictated, as it were, by a narrator and corrected by the author. Third-person stories, by their very different stances, pretend to emphasize events directly rather than the ways and means of telling a tale. It becomes very important, then, for writer and reader of a first-person story to negotiate early on and to determine two related conditions: (1) is the story considered to be mainly written or spoken? and (2) where is the narrator now, and how much time has passed since the events here recounted have transpired?

Gatsby is barely underway before we learn (in the fourth paragraph) that this is intended as a written rather than a spoken version of the tale, and, indeed, that it is a *book*, presumably the same book that we are here and now reading: "Gatsby, the man who gives his name to this book" (p. 2). This assumption raises another question, one whose resolution is held in abeyance (suspense) for quite some time. As far as the narrator is concerned, as stated clearly in the opening paragraphs, the events of the story are all over and done with. Things have happened. The teller has experienced them, reacted to them, and in some ways been changed by them. It is all after the fact. But there are various elements of the telling of the story that are clearly in the present tense. Some are merely aphoristic, reactions that have become generalizations and link the time of telling directly with the time of happening: "Again a sort of apology arose to my lips. Almost any exhibition of complete self-sufficiency draws a stunned tribute from me" (p. 11). Or (for instance): "There is no confusion like the confusion of a simple mind, and as we drove away Tom was feeling the hot whips of panic" (p. 149). There are many of these present judgments of past actions. And there are other occasions, at regular intervals throughout, when the narrator interrupts past action to assert an act of present memory: "Among the broken fragments of the last five minutes at table I remember the candles being lit again, pointlessly, and I was conscious of wanting to look squarely at every one, and yet to avoid all eyes" (p. 19). Or: "I think [*now*, evidently and distinctly from *then*] he'd tanked up a good deal at luncheon, and his determination to have my company bordered on violence" (p. 28). And: "But I am slow-thinking and full of interior rules that act as brakes on my desires, and I knew that first I had to get myself definitely out of that tangle back home" (p. 72).

At the risk of being crudely obvious, I call attention to two elements above and beyond the functional value that these recurring time shifts – between the time of the events described and the time of the composition of their description – have, by keeping the reader conscious of the two separate but simultaneous time schemes. The first of these is to focus our attention on aftermath, to emphasize reaction more than action. The second characteristic is to set in some sense of tension, if not conflict, often within the same sentence, the qualities of the spoken versus the written American language.

Gatsby is a marvelous experiment, a triumph of the *written* American vernacular, the range, suppleness, and eloquence of it. But for the written vernacular language of the times to be fully explored, it was necessary to set it in direct contrast to the spoken language, not only in the contrast between credible dialogue in the dramatic scenes, but, occasionally and within limits, in the narration itself: thus "out of that tangle back home" and "I think he'd tanked up a good deal at luncheon. . . ." In other words, the written narration, this *book* by Nick Carraway, has to touch, however briefly, on the level of spoken narration in order to define itself clearly. Moreover, this capability is necessary if full use is to be made of the spoken vernacular in dramatic and satirical scenes. The overall effect, the created language of this book, Nick Carraway's language, offers up a full range between lyrical evocation and depths of feeling at one end and casual, if hard-knuckled, matters of fact. It allows for the poetry of intense perception to live simultaneously and at ease with a hard-edged, implaccable vulgarity. Each draws strength from the conflict with the other.

This same tension of time and language is at the center of Carraway's point of view and is expressed early on in Chapter 2 as Carraway, drunk, imagines himself as a stranger capable of including even Carraway as an object in his speculative vision: "Yet high over the city our line of yellow windows must have contributed their share of human secrecy to the casual watcher in the darkening streets, and I was him too, looking up and wondering. I was within and without, simultaneously enchanted and repelled by the inexhaustible variety of life" (p. 43). *I was within and without. . . .* *Gatsby* becomes an intricate demonstration of that kind of complex double vision, of the *process* of it. We are not far into the story (Chapter 3) before we discover that the "book" Nick Carraway mentioned at the outset, the book that, completed, will turn out to be *The Great Gatsby*, is not yet finished, is in the process of being written. "Reading over what I have written so far, I see I have given the impression that the events of three nights several weeks apart were all that absorbed me" (p. 68). This additional sense of time (narrator pauses to reread what he has written so far) almost, not quite, allows for another kind of time level – the time of revision. At least it asserts that what is being reported has been carefully thought about and can be corrected if need be. And at the least, it makes the time of the composition of the story closely parallel to the reader's left-to-right, chronological adventure.

A bit later, in a number of ways, we are encouraged to *participate* actively in the narrative process as, for example in Chapter six, where Carraway explains and defends a narrative choice:

> He told me all this very much later, but I've put it down here with the idea of exploding those first wild rumors about his antecedents, which weren't even faintly true. Moreover he told it to me at a time of confusion, when I had reached the point of believing everything and nothing about him. So I take advantage of this short halt, while Gatsby, so to speak, caught his breath, to clear this set of misconceptions away. (pp. 121–2)

Here the focus is so clearly on the process of making and of the free, if pragmatic, choices involved that the reader is strongly reminded of the story as artifact, although, ironically, it is Carraway's selective virtuosity that at once supersedes and disguises Fitzgerald's.

Meanwhile, narrative virtuosity becomes increasingly various and complex as we move deeper into the story. In Chapter 4 we are given a first-person narration, in her own words, by Jordan Baker, "sitting up very straight on a straight chair in the tea-garden at the Plaza Hotel" (p. 89), concerning Daisy and Gatsby in 1917. This is told in a credible and appropriate vernacular for Jordan Baker – as recalled, of course, by Carraway. More romantic and lyrical by far is Gatsby's own story, which is told (out of sequence) in indirect discourse. Carraway finds a third-person high style appropriate to the inner mystery and turmoil of the young (and mostly nonverbal) Gatsby. By this time, Carraway so dominates the material of the story (even his speculation and tentativeness can be taken as the authority of integrity) that he is

112

capable of creating a language that can dramatize in rhythmic images the inward and spiritual condition of Gatsby as a young man:

> But his heart was in a constant, turbulent riot. The most grotesque and fantastic conceits haunted him in his bed at night. A universe of ineffable gaudiness spun itself out in his brain while the clock ticked on the washstand and the moon soaked with wet light his tangled clothes upon the floor. Each night he added to the pattern of his fancies until drowsiness closed down upon some vivid scene with an oblivious embrace. For a while these reveries provided an outlet for his imagination; they were a satisfactory hint of the unreality of reality, a promise that the rock of the world was founded securely on a fairy's wing. (p. 119)

In Chapter 7, another form of indirect discourse, this time a third-person account of the death of Myrtle Wilson, matter of fact and vaguely journalistic (as if, as is later implied, its source were indeed the newspapers), is employed. "The young Greek, Michaelis, who ran the coffee joint beside the ashheaps was the principal witness at the inquest. He had slept through the heat until after five, when he strolled over to the garage, and found George Wilson sick in his office – really sick, pale as his own pale hair and shaking all over" (pp. 163–4). Carraway returns to this place – "Now I want to go back a little and tell what happened at the garage after we left there the night before" (p. 187) – out of chronological sequence, in Chapter 8, with an almost purely dramatic third-person omniscient scene, which, in any literal sense, has to be wholly *imagined* by Carraway, but which offers brief moments of sensory perception and thought by both Michaelis and George Wilson. Stylistically, this unit is quite distinct, as is Carraway's imagined version of Gatsby's last moments, here quite candidly blending overt speculation with an implausible certainty to form a single poetic vision:

> He must have looked up at an unfamiliar sky through frightening leaves and shivered as he found what a grotesque thing a rose is and how raw the sunlight was upon the scarcely created grass. A new world, material without being real, where poor ghosts, breathing dreams like air, drifted fortuitously about . . . like that ashen, fantastic figure gliding toward him through the amorphous trees. (p. 194)

This high moment is a direct reversal of the more usual pattern of perception in the book, in which the sight of the ashen figure (Wilson) might have led him next to react with a generalized vision of "poor ghosts, breathing dreams like air." Here, at the last moment of his life, Gatsby, as conceived and imagined by Carraway reverses reality and unreality, just as Carraway himself had done earlier, imagining himself as a stranger in the street staring up at lit windows and wondering. The result of the reversal is something close to prescience, certainly something stronger than premonition.

Finally, this extension of style to the extreme, almost absurd edge of narrative credibility allows Carraway the indulgence of imagining direct, and quite vernacular, dialogue from the dead Gatsby:

> But, as they drew back the sheet and looked at Gatsby with un-moved eyes, his protest continued in my brain:
> "Look here, old sport, you've got to get somebody for me. You've got to try hard. I can't go through this alone." (p. 198)

In point of fact, stylistically *Gatsby* is a complicated composite of several distinct kinds of prose, set within the boundaries of a written narration, a composite style whose chief demonstrable point appears to be the inadequacy of any single style (or single means of perception, point of view) by itself to do justice to the story. Which is a story of a world not so much in transition as falling apart without realizing it. New and old clash continually, violently. It is shown to be impossible to escape the one by embracing the other. Carraway, as is his habit, finds an aphorism for precisely this paradox, seeking to explain "the colossal vitality" of Gatsby's illusion: "No amount of fire or freshness can challenge what a man will store up in his ghostly heart" (p. 116).

Nick Carraway's authority, and his insistence on telling his own story together with Gatsby's — and it should be remembered that it is Carraway who gets the last aphoristic and poetic word, who presents the haunting image of "the green light, the orgastic future that year by year recedes before us" even as we are swept back-ward like "boats against the current, borne back ceaselessly into the past" (p. 218) — is to establish a powerful, if illusory, sense of unity that tends to camouflage the variety and complexity of the narration. French critic André Le Vot, in the chapters of his recent biography of Fitzgerald that deal with *Gatsby*, creates an elegant and impressive paradigm of the use of color symbolism and the constant use of light and dark in the story, contrived to hold the discrete parts of the story, in the subtext at least, in a conventional unified coherence. These things seem to work well for that purpose; and there are other elements and patterns that tend to serve roughly the same purpose, all adding up to an impression of unified style. Beneath the surface, however, *Gatsby* is boiling with conflict – chiefly the conflict of new and old, the inadequacy of the old ways and means to deal with the new world of the twentieth century. Thus, behind its seemingly bland and polite surface, *Gatsby* is, in many ways, a wildly experimental novel, a trying out of what would become familiar, if more varied, strategies of our serious literature and, especially, of the range of our literary language.

With all of its apparent acknowledgment of the power of the past, *Gatsby* is a leap toward the future, the invention of new styles, therefore the dead end of something else. Those wonderful letters the young Fitzgerald received from literary dignitaries at the time are explicit in announcing this. "You are creating the contemporary world much as Thackeray did his in *Pendennis* and *Vanity Fair*," Gertrude Stein wrote, "and this isn't a bad compliment."[2] T. S. Eliot called it, accurately, "the first step that American fiction has taken since Henry James."[3] And Edith Wharton, wisely, felt threatened. She had a minor criticism, based on traditional practices: "My present quarrel with you is only this: that to make Gatsby really Great, you ought to have given us his early career . . . instead of a short résumé of it. That would have situated him, & made his final tragedy a tragedy instead of a 'fait divers' for the morning papers.

"But you'll tell me that's the old way, & consequently not *your* way."[4]

In terms of form, then, more than anything else, in terms of *style*, *Gatsby* is a pioneering novel. Other masters of the first half of this century may have done more radical and extraordinary things with the novel's shape and substance, but, by and large, these other great books were (are), at the least, inimitable. With *Gatsby*,

Fitzgerald advanced the form of the American novel for the benefit of all American novelists who have followed after him, whether they know it or not. They seem to sense this, to bear witness to it, in their continuing admiration for *Gatsby*. For youthful romance, it is hard to beat *This Side of Paradise*. For the purity of nostalgia and the evocation of a period, an era, there is always my old favorite, *Tender Is the Night*. But in *Gatsby*, which pretends to be a little of both, youthful romance and nostalgic period piece, it is a matter of style; and that style is for all our bitter seasons.

NOTES

1 "Three Letters about *The Great Gatsby*," *The Crack-Up*, ed. Edmund Wilson (New York: New Directions, 1945), p. 309.
2 Ibid., p. 308.
3 Ibid., p. 310.
4 Ibid., p. 309.

Notes on Contributors

Richard Anderson teaches English at Huntingdon College in Montgomery, Alabama. His publications include several articles on F. Scott Fitzgerald.

Matthew J. Bruccoli is Jefferies Professor of English at the University of South Carolina. A leading authority on Fitzgerald, he is the author of *Some Sort of Epic Grandeur: The Life of F. Scott Fitzgerald*.

Kenneth E. Eble is Professor of English at the University of Utah. His revised edition of *F. Scott Fitzgerald* was published by Twayne Publishers in 1977.

George Garrett, poet and novelist, is Henry Hoyns Professor of Creative Writing at the University of Virginia.

Roger Lewis, who has published a novel and a volume of poetry, directs a small publishing company in Washington, D.C. He is an Associate Professor of English at George Mason University.

Susan Resneck Parr is Dean of the College of Arts and Sciences at the University of Tulsa. She is the author of *The Moral of the Story: Literature, Values, and American Education* and of numerous articles about modern literature.

Selected Bibliography

The standard text of *The Great Gatsby* is the first printing by Scribners (New York, 1925). For scholarly purposes this text should be supplemented by Matthew J. Bruccoli's *Apparatus for F. Scott Fitzgerald's The Great Gatsby* (Columbia, S.C.: University of South Carolina Press, 1974).

Special Journals
Fitzgerald Newsletter (1958–68). Washington, D.C.: Microcard Editions, 1969.
Fitzgerald/Hemingway Annual (1969–79). Washington, D.C.: Microcard Editions, 1969–76; Detroit: Bruccoli Clark/Gale Research, 1977–79.

Bibliographies
Bruccoli, Matthew J. *F. Scott Fitzgerald: A Descriptive Bibliography.* Pittsburgh: University of Pittsburgh Press, 1972. *Supplement.* University of Pittsburgh Press, 1980. Primary.
Bryer, Jackson R. *The Critical Reputation of F. Scott Fitzgerald.* Hamden, Conn: Archon, 1967. *Supplement One.* Hamden, Conn: Archon, 1984. Secondary.

Textual Studies
Bruccoli, Matthew J. *Apparatus for F. Scott Fitzgerald's The Great Gatsby.* Columbia: University of South Carolina Press, 1974.
Crosland, Andrew T. *A Concordance to F. Scott Fitzgerald's The Great Gatsby.* Detroit: Bruccoli Clark/Gale Research, 1975.
The Great Gatsby: A Facsimile of the Manuscript, ed. Matthew J. Bruccoli. Washington, D.C.: Bruccoli Clark/Microcard, 1973.

Other
Bryer, Jackson R. "Four Decades of Fitzgerald Studies: The Best and the Brightest," *Twentieth Century Literature* 26 (Summer 1980): 247–67.

Long, Robert Emmet. *The Achieving of The Great Gatsby.* Lewisburg, Pa: Bucknell University Press, 1979.

Tanselle, G. Thomas, and Bryer, Jackson R. *"The Great Gatsby* — A Study in Literary Reputation," *New Mexico Quarterly* 33 (Winter 1963–4):409–25.

Whitley, J. S. *F. Scott Fitzgerald: The Great Gatsby.* London: Edward Arnold, 1976.

Collections of Essays

Bryer, Jackson R., ed. *F. Scott Fitzgerald: The Critical Reception.* New York: Franklin, 1978.

Hoffman, Frederick J., ed. *The Great Gatsby: A Study.* New York: Scribners, 1962.

Lockridge, Ernest, ed. *Twentieth Century Interpretations of The Great Gatsby.* Englewood Cliffs, N.J.: Prentice-Hall, 1968.

Piper, Henry Dan, ed. *Fitzgerald's The Great Gatsby.* New York: Scribners, 1970.